Tempus ORAL HISTORY *Series*

voices of
Southborough
and High Brooms

Victoria Road, Southborough.

Penticost's cows on the Common.

Cover illustration: *St Peter's School, Southborough, 11 March 1966. (*Courier *photograph)*

Tempus ORAL HISTORY *Series*

voices of
Southborough
and High Brooms

Compiled by
Chris McCooey

TEMPUS

First published 2000
Copyright © Chris McCooey, 2000

Tempus Publishing Limited
The Mill, Brimscombe Port,
Stroud, Gloucestershire, GL5 2QG

ISBN 0 7524 2054 2

Typesetting and origination by
Tempus Publishing Limited
Printed in Great Britain by
Midway Clark Printing, Wiltshire

The coat of arms of Southborough and High Brooms. The ram's head represents weaving, the two rectangles are bricks, the circle is a cricket ball, the two bushes are broom, which gives its name to High Brooms, and the oak is the Bounds Oak.

Contents

Introduction

I have enjoyed working on this book. It gives me pleasure to record the reminiscences, the anecdotes, the stories and memories of people who have lived locally. Hopefully it is their authentic voice that comes through, their turn of phrase, their wry comment, their humour. My job was just to get it down on paper so that others can say: 'Of course, I remember that,' and 'Oh yes, old So-and-So,' and be led off down a memory lane of their own.

So many people have helped me on this project, in particular those whose voices can be heard on the succeeding pages. Each and every one is named in the text and to all of them I would like to say a big 'thank you'; it was a privilege for me to be given your time and to record your thoughts. It was particularly enjoyable when a group of old friends from schooldays, or colleagues from work, got together (with me and my notebook present) and they recalled events and people from their past. One memory seemed to lead, usually happily and easily, to another, and a good time was had by all.

Apart from the people in the book itself, I would like to thank a number of other people personally. Over the years, the Southborough Society has published several accounts of people's early memories of Southborough and High Brooms and I have used a number of these, mostly verbatim. Although some of these accounts were written some time ago their voices come through clearly and they do have a story to tell. I am very grateful to Fiona Woodfield, the chairman of the Society, as well as Maxwell Macfarlane and John Kennedy, the main Society archivists, for making all the Society's past publications and material available to me, as well as their photographs and pictures.

I am also indebted to the *Kent & Sussex Courier* which has supplied a number of the photographs that are in the book, including the cover illustration. Street shots, people shots, special events were all often first recorded by our local paper which is such an important source of any local history. The editor, Martin Oxley, and Frank Chapman, who writes the Warwick column, have been most generous in their free use of the material from the paper and to allow me to use their Letters Page to publicize the project and to get original material that otherwise would have remained in a single memory or boxed away in an attic.

As ever when you rely on memory, I'm sure there are a number of mistakes – a mis-spelt name here, a date wrong there. For these I apologize; but if you let me know what they are, I will endeavour to correct them for any future edition.

So, over to you, the reader. There are all sorts for your delectation. Events both momentous and mundane, great joy and tragedy, sadness at a life cut short, rejoicing at a life of service and giving to others, fond memories, poignant memories, good times, and not so good, recalled by a cross section of the people of Southborough and High Brooms. People like you and me.

Chris McCooey, Modest Corner, Southborough. May 2000.

CHAPTER 1

Early Times

The Weavers today.

The Health Resort

Dr E. Paget Thurstan, *formerly Obstetric Physician to the Marylebone General Hospital in London, retired to live in Southborough sometime in the 1880s. He was a member of Southborough Local Board, a predecessor of the Town Council, and in 1885 he wrote a treatise:* Southborough, its Chalybeate Springs, Climate and Attractions as a Health Resort. *The book's purpose was to publicize and promote the attractions of Southborough as a residential location, particularly for those seeking a climate suitable for convalescence or maintaining a healthy lifestyle. He writes:*

The town is situated on the crest of a ridge composed of sandy soil. Rain water drains away quickly, leaving the ground dry, and this type of environment gives rise to fewer diseases and ailments than places where the ground stays wet. Southborough

The pumping station at Southborough waterworks, c. 1919.

is over 500ft above sea level and the atmospheric pressure is therefore less here than it is at lower levels. This difference is plainly appreciated by delicate persons.

The exhilarating Southborough air is pure, because of the abundance throughout the district of foliage, which produces life-giving oxygen. Indeed, the eminent physician Sir William Gull once stood on Southborough Common and said: 'It is impossible in any part of the world to breathe purer air.' Although there have been problems with water in the past, the new mains which carry water from the pumping station at Bentham Hill mean that the water now is of excellent quality for drinking, and being very soft, is well adapted for washing and steam purposes. In addition, the chalybeate spring at Stemps Farm [now the Weavers] produces iron water as good for medicinal use as that produced at the Pantiles. Southborough

receives above average sunshine and generally fair weather, with the result that the average age at death is higher here than in all other West Kent sanitary districts, except for Tenterden.

A wealth of information is provided by the good doctor. A night's accommodation in the Coffee Tavern (now the sub-aqua shop on the corner of Western Road and London Road) cost ninepence. A journey by horse drawn omnibus to Tunbridge Wells cost fourpence. Tennis, archery, bowls and quoits were available on land adjoining Christ Church (now the grounds of the Primary School in Broomhill Park Road). The better-off sections of society devoted much time to riding, picnicking, boating at Tonbridge and hunting.

There was a selection of horse-drawn transport available for hire. This ranged from First Class (two horses with a driver and up to five passengers at 1s 6d for the first mile plus sixpence for each additional half mile) to Third Class (two passengers drawn by a pony, mule or ass – eightpence for the first mile and each additional half mile fourpence). Bath chairs drawn by hand were also available.

With regard to the social makeup of the town, the doctor observes:

The better classes in Southborough are composed of retired military and naval men, clergymen of private means, gentlemen of moderate private fortune as well as professional and medical men and schoolmasters. [But] the hamlet known as High Brooms ... consists solely of cottages occupied by employees of the High Brooms Brickworks and the Tunbridge Wells Gas Company. These residents have neglected their sanitary conditions which has caused an increase in sickness and raised the death-rate in the hamlet. For the benefit of those people unfortunate enough to be in even worse circumstances, Southborough is endowed with a soup kitchen and various charitable groups, including one which specializes in producing blankets.

Dr Thurstan was very much involved in the public life of Southborough and was keen to see the town compete for the custom of visitors with the nearby more famous resort of Tunbridge Wells. Although he does not state so categorically, it would seem that the official opening of the Bentham Hill Waterworks just a few weeks prior to publication was the book's main inspiration. It occurred to the doctor that the final obstacle to Southborough becoming a celebrated health resort had been overcome at last, and this highly-motivated Southborough citizen could now with a clear conscience set out, as he put it, to 'whet the appetite of strangers'.

William Weekes

Betty Evans lives in Manor Road.

My great-grandfather was William Weekes and he was the farm bailiff to Sir David Salomons and lived in the bailiff's cottage which was Lady's Gift Farm house. I have a photograph of him wearing a smock – I still have the smock.

My great-uncle Thomas and my grandfather, also called William, used to go to the Holme School at Windy Edge, near the present-day Birchwood Garage. They would walk to school but would set off early so that they could do some work at the Hand and Sceptre before lessons began. They used to clean knives and shoes and earned threepence a week which helped towards the school fees. They had two sisters, Esther and Elizabeth, but they went to Speldhurst which was one of the first free church schools in the area. Naturally they walked both ways, usually through the hop fields from Kibbles Lane to Speldhurst Mill. When my great-grandfather was bailiff and he had finished his daily work early, Sir David would tell him to put some hay on the floor of the wagon and drive it to Speldhurst and bring the schoolchildren home to Southborough.

My father Herbert went to see Sir David Salomons, along with half of Southborough, when he drove the first car back to Broomhill Park. There was a man waving a red flag going in front of the car. As Sir David drove along London Road, he noticed my father and stopped the car to give him a ride, so he became the first person in Southborough to be driven in a car.

Great-grandfather William died in 1917 and he is buried in Southborough Cemetery. I remember on a Friday afternoon we used to

William Weekes (great-grandfather of Betty Evans) was Bailiff to Sir David Salomons. He lived in Lady's Gift Farm house and died in 1917.

go over to the cemetery and put flowers on his grave. We used to call in on Mr and Mrs Harris who lived in Wood Cottage on Victoria Road. Mr Harris was the grave digger and he used to let me pick the daisies in the cemetery which seemed that much bigger than other daisies.

My great aunt Alice, married to great uncle Bill, used to make meringues for Miss Sayer's Tea Room on London Road (it was later Jon Hoff's the jeweller's and now is a hairdresser's). She used to put them in the oven at night and in the morning when the fire had gone out they were ready. Us kids always hoped that one or two would break so that we could eat them. Lady's Gift Farm house was pulled down when they built the council houses sometime in the 1950s.

Fiona Woodfield, the current chairman of the Southborough Society, has done some research on Lady's Gift Farm and tells how a Tudor lady's gift is recalled in a Southborough street name.

Elizabeth Darrell was a daughter of the Lord of the Manor of Horsmonden. Like so many families, the Darrells had received the lordship of the manor as a gift from Henry VIII. Elizabeth's father was Chief Clerk to the Royal Kitchen and her maternal grandfather had the mysterious-sounding title of Clerk of the Green Cloth – surely nothing to do with billiards?

Elizabeth was married twice, first to the widower Henry Nevill, sixth Lord Abergavenny, remembered for quelling the rebellion of Thomas Wyatt against Mary Tudor in 1554. After his death, Lady Abergavenny was evidently comfortably off and mindful of the needs of the less fortunate, and appears to have founded Lady Abergavenny's Charity at the time. Later she married William Sedley of Aylesford,

Wood Cottage, c. 1960.

11

who was created a baronet in 1611. When she died, around 1618, Lady Sedley (as she had become) left money and jewellery worth a total of £531 for the relief of poor families in Horsmonden.

In 1619, the five churchwardens and overseers of the poor in Horsmonden were able to buy two farms, one at Ticehurst and the other in Speldhurst Road, Southborough, which back then was the 'south borough' of the parish of Tonbridge. The Southborough land was purchased from a local gentleman, Alexander Thomas, and comprised 'two pieces called Clarke's and five pieces called Doolgardens containing 17 acres, the Houlden Land of 6 acres and the Doubles of 12 acres.' The purchase of the farm house followed some years later.

According to the Listed Building description compiled in 1949, the farmhouse was a small two-storey building, probably constructed in the seventeenth century. It was built of bricks at ground floor level, with weatherboards on the front elevation, tile hanging on the side walls, a half-hipped tiled roof and casement windows. In 1792 the historian Edward Hasted recorded that Lady's Gift Farm was yielding to Horsmonden's Lady Abergavenny Charity the sum of £19 16s 5d. Together with the rent from the other farm, the combined sum was able to relieve fifty poor residents in Horsmonden on a regular basis and a further twenty in a more casual, one-off way.

At the end of the eighteenth century, the tenant farmer was John Pack and he had to go to Horsmonden in person to pay his rent 'at the house of the Widow Foreman, being the sign of the Gun' (now the Gun and Spitroast pub).

By 1842, when the tithe map and apportionment was drawn up, the farm was known as Horsmonden Charity Farm and was 40 acres in size. All the original field names had changed and were now called names like Horsmonden Meadow, Hilly Field, Muddy Field and Crossway Field. The farm extended roughly where Lady's Gift Road, Brightridge and Keel Gardens lie today, abutting the north side of Speldhurst Road to a point opposite Broomhill Road, but with two fields on the south side of Speldhurst Road, at the end of the present-day Kibbles Lane.

On 10 November 1887, the farm was sold to the owners of the adjoining properties in two portions: one portion to Sir David Salomons, hence the Weekes family living in the farmhouse, and the other to Mr Robert Pott of Bentham Hill House. The trustees of the Horsmonden Charity presumably found better means of investing their capital than administering a tenant farm. In the later part of the twentieth century the old farmhouse was demolished and most of the land was used for housing. One portion of Lady's Gift Farm that was not built on but is still used for crops (albeit not the hops and arable crops of days gone by) is the Town Council's allotments abutting Speldhurst Road and Bright Ridge.

Trotty Veck

Mason Coker, who for many years ran a printing business in Bedford Road, discovered a connection that Southborough had with the great Victorian writer Charles Dickens.

A certain Mr Beck had some employment in St Peter's church on the Common. He seems to have been part-time at this place – he may have stoked the boiler, polished the brass and done sundry other odd jobs. One of his duties was to sweep, several times a day, the 'crossing' somewhere between Pennington Road and Victoria Road. This was in the second half of the nineteenth century, when there were numerous horses travelling the road. You can guess that this was an important job when the ladies wore long dresses.

Mr Beck could always be found between one and two o'clock, sitting on the steps in the porch of the Imperial Hotel. He used to spread a cloth on part of the step, where his daughter brought him his dinner. He had a 'sideline' in that he was a messenger: one could hand him an envelope or a parcel to be delivered locally, say, Tunbridge Wells or Frant. Mr Beck was always in a hurry and seemed to have an unusual gait, which made him appear to be always 'trotting', so he acquired the nickname 'Trotty'.

Charles Dickens visited Southborough on occasion and could not help but notice this man who seemed always to be trotting somewhere. Dickens wrote a story called *Chimes*, which is set in Southborough's St Peter's church: the principal character is 'Trotty Veck'. Dickens paid Mr Beck one guinea for the use of his name and character in that story, changing Beck to Veck. Mr Beck's great-great-grandson, Tony Streeter, lives in Yew Tree Road.

The Hand and Sceptre Hotel, Southborough, c. 1890. (Courier photograph)

Charge of the Light Brigade

Frank Chapman, who writes the Warwick column for the Kent & Sussex Courier, *recorded the story of a Southborough man who had been present at one of the most famous battles in history.*

Albert Mitchell was a private and, later, a sergeant in the 13th Light Dragoons and fought throughout the Crimean War, including taking part in the Charge of the Light Brigade at Balaclava. He wrote a book about his experiences – *Recollections of One of the Light Brigade* – which was printed by Richard Pelton of Tunbridge Wells and published privately in 1884. In the opinion of historians, it remains one of the finest accounts of the famous charge, principally because it was written by a private soldier.

For discipline and red-blooded courage under fire, the charge of the horsemen towards the Russian guns, one and a half miles away at the head of a valley, has never been surpassed. Of the 607 horsemen who took part in the twenty-minute engagement, 197 were killed and 80 were wounded. The carnage among the horses was terrible, and many hardened troopers wept, not for themselves or their comrades so much as for the mounts they loved.

Mitchell records: 'A corporal riding beside me was hit full in the face by a shell and all around me the ranks were being continually thinned by gunfire from left, right and in front, felling three or four horses at a time. Up to this time I was going on all right but missed my left-hand man from the side and, thinking it might soon be my turn, I offered up a short prayer: "Oh Lord, protect me and watch over my poor mother." We were now very close to the guns, for we were entering the smoke which hung in clouds in front of them.

I could see some of the gunners running from the front to the rear when just at that moment a shell from the battery on the right struck my horse, carrying away the shoulder and part of the chest, and exploded a few yards off. Fortunately I was on the ground when it exploded, or some of the fragments would most likely have reached me. On my recovery from the shock I found my horse was lying on his left side. My left leg was beneath him and my right above him. I tried to move but just at that moment heard the second line come galloping towards where I lay and fully expected to be trampled on. I looked up and saw it was the 4th Light Dragoons.

I called out, "For God's sake, don't ride over me!" Whether they heard it or not, I shall never know. God must have been able to hear and He most mercifully answered my prayers, for He guided them over me so that not a hoof touched a hair of my head. To Him alone be all honour and praise for his manifold mercies to me.

After a struggle I managed to free my leg and stood up, sword in hand. There was a hail of bullets from the enemy and a fellow trooper pulled me down and we sheltered behind the dead horse. After a while, fearing that we would be taken prisoner, we headed back down the valley through the litter of dead and dying men and horses. I found my left-hand man. He was terribly wounded and all I could do was make him comfortable with a drink of rum and water but I could see death on his countenance.'

William Howard Russell, *The Times* correspondent, who watched the charge

In

Memory of
ALBERT MITCHELL,
LATE SERGEANT 13TH HUSSARS
AND OF THE KENT COUNTY CONSTABULARY
DIED 16TH JANUARY 1897,
AGED 67 YEARS.

DECEASED SERVED THROUGHOUT THE CRIMEAN CAMPAIG
TAKING PART IN THE ENGAGEMENTS AT ALMA,
BALACLAVA, INKERMANN, AND SIEGE OF SEBASTOPOL
ALSO THE AFFAIRS OF THE
BULGANAK AND MACKENZIES FARM.

THIS STONE WAS ERECTED
BY THE MEMBERS OF THE ABOVE CORPS
AS A TRIBUTE OF RESPECT
TO A BRAVE AND DESERVING COMRADE.

Albert Mitchell's grave in St Peter's churchyard. He was a soldier in the 13th Light Dragoons in 1854, and took part in the Charge of the Light Brigade. The regiment later changed its name to Hussars.

from a safe distance, wrote in his despatch: 'When at last the guns went silent and the smoke was drifting from the valley, all that could be heard was the melancholy thud of the farriers' pistols as they went about despatching wounded horses.'

The Crimea, in which Britain blundered into war against Russia, with the old enemy France as her most unlikely ally, has been described as this country's most futile and pointless military adventure. The Charge of the Light Brigade was one of many dreadful blunders. It was never intended to happen, but it did. The fact that some of the officers principally concerned were consumed by jealousy, and/or were not speaking to each other, was largely to blame.

After the war, Mitchell became a policeman in the Kent County Constabulary and served for many years at Cranbrook until he contracted Bright's disease [a kidney infection named after the physician Richard Bright who first diagnosed it while working in Guy's Hospital in the 1820s]. He was forced to retire in 1884 with a pension of 13s a week. Lord Cranbrook made him a steward of the St George's Club, but by 1892 the old soldier had to give this up and he retired to live in Southborough, first at 20 Norton Road, then, when his health began to fail, with his sister, at 2 Taylor Street (his wife had predeceased him in 1875).

In January 1897 a retired officer, Col. L.A. White, of 133 Upper Grosvenor Road in Tunbridge Wells, concerned about former Sergeant Mitchell's personal circumstances, joined with Dr Gilbert, his GP, in calling a public meeting to open a fund for the old Crimean War veteran. Donations came in and the committee booked the Great Hall for a concert at which Tennyson's poem *The Charge of the Light Brigade* would be recited.

But it was all too late. Within a few days Mitchell was dead, aged sixty-seven. The War Office had refused him aid because he 'was not in absolute distress.' The man, who had been noted for his physique – he went right through the Crimean campaign without a day's sickness – still had the relic of a tremendous sword arm, 'still of a span many soldiers would be proud of,' the *Courier* reported.

His body was laid out in a coffin and it was taken from Taylor Street to St Peter's church on the Common. The cortège was headed by the local Yeomanry (volunteer cavalry) and Volunteers (infantry). Four sergeants from the 13th Hussars acted as guards and twenty policemen escorted the Union Jack-draped coffin mounted on the manual fire engine of Tunbridge Wells Volunteer Brigade.

CHAPTER 2

People and Places

A horse-drawn bus waiting in front of Stuart Cottage, c. 1910. (Courier photograph).

Working Horses

George Paine was born in Southborough in 1904. His father was a respected member of the local community, being a magistrate and farmer as well as Chairman of Southborough Urban District Council from 1908 to 1910. Later George's father became a baker. As a young person growing up in Southborough, George remembers how important horses were as transport for the local businesses as well as for farm work.

My earliest childhood memories are inevitably coloured by the fact that life was shared with the working horse. The forge,

the wheelwright's shop, the stables, not to mention the bakehouse and the furnace room, all contrived by scent and sound to create a back-drop against which we lived our lives.

I recall the clip-clop of hooves echoing along St John's Road, known then, for some reason as 'The Lew'. When we were taken to shop in Tunbridge Wells, it was considered most profligate to take the horse-bus both ways. The horse-bus company plied from Southborough Common to the Central Station. A trace horse used to be hitched in front of the regular pair to help them up the two hills, then at the Fountain he was released to await the next bus. On Quarry

St John's Road, looking from Powdermill Lane towards Tunbridge Wells, early twentieth century.

Hill, Tonbridge, there was a trace horse maintained by the Dumb Friends' League. Often a carter would wait at the bottom of the hill for help with his load, and a few coppers in the box fixed to the harness of the helpful friend would leave everyone happy.

Tunbridge Wells a hundred years ago must have had rather more than an average horse-drawn population. There were the mansions of the wealthy newcomers, sharing a common stretch of park land, each with a lodge-gate cottage, mews and stables at the back to house the coachmen and others whose job was to see to the family transport. This would consist of the coach and pair, the brougham and perhaps a trap or governess cart for the lady of the house. There were also big houses of the local landed gentry, each with its quota of horse-drawn vehicles, the gentlemen farmers, the

tenant farmers, doctors, parsons and prosperous tradesmen, all depending on some form of suitable turn-out. These, with the hunters and racehorses, were the aristocrats. Then, of course, there was that less glamorous horse population – the four-legged workers – from the magnificent Shires and Clydesdales on the farms to the hacks at the livery stables and the helots between the shafts of the tradesmen's vans. All this meant plenty of work for the farrier, the blacksmith, the wheelwright, coach builder, corn merchant, veterinary surgeon and a host of others.

In the bakery yard at the back of our house in Holden Park Road, we stabled seven or eight working horses. Adjoining was Mr William Carter's forge in, naturally, Forge Road, run by Bill, the son, and his father with one good eye and a blank socket from a mishap with a live spark. Nearby, the wheelwright, Mr Stonham, a childhood hero with the deepest bass voice I have ever known, was a magician when working oak, ash, beech, elm with the simplest of tools and certainly no mechanical aids beyond an ancient hand-propelled lathe.

What a hissing and scraping and a brushing was there in the cobbled yard every Sunday morning as, with curry comb and dandy brush, the ponies would be made ready for a smart turn-out on Monday morning. Vans were washed, hooves black-leaded, and in icy conditions roughs were screwed in to the horses' shoes.

I could not have been more than eight or nine years old when I was allowed to watch our vet, Mr Chalmers, perform a tracheotomy on a youngish cob to improve his breathing. One grand old four-legged gentleman, who suffered from rheumatism, could never be allowed to lie down in his stall. He was always suspended by two wide-banded slings raised by a rope across the rafters. Each morning two men would let him gently down and, after a short while, he could do a good day's work with the rest of them.

What a proud moment it was when I was handed the halter rope of a pony who was suffering from the 'gripes'. The instructions were to keep walking him continuously round the neighbouring roads. If he was allowed to stop, death would follow, whether of me or the pony I was never quite sure. There was an even prouder moment when, at about the age of twelve, I was

The Paine Smith bakery at the corner of Speldhurst Road and London Road.

trusted to take a horse and van onto the high road for the first time. That occasion of indescribable bliss was due to the non-delivery of yeast for bread-making, and I had to collect two buckets of brewer's balm yeast from Kelsey's Brewery opposite St John's church. I have often wondered if the bread that day could have had a specially interesting flavour for the teetotal old ladies.

A lively little grey mare, fresh from a month out to grass, gave me quite an adventure. During the long school holiday, I was given a country round in the Langton and Groombridge area. The last few customers were in Speldhurst, the very last being the Taylors at the mill house, where Mr Bryant used to live. At a never-to-be-forgotten spot near the top of the hill, the little mare decided to bolt for home, probably as a protest gallop against my handling. We bucketed full tilt down the hill, missed the bridge parapet by inches and then, with some rather bad-tempered encouragement from me, she was made to run up the next hill and so home to arrive in the yard in a muck sweat, accompanied by some highly-coloured expressions of disapproval from the rounds foreman. My penance was to return and finish the round ignominiously on a trade bicycle.

We had three meadows, still called the 'lost' meadows, buried in the heart of Brokes Wood, just below where I used to live on the Ridgewaye. Grass for a resting pony was always in demand. Ponies were often exchanged and sent to our other bakery in Maidstone. The simplest way to effect a transfer was for a lad to ride the horse along the tow path from Tonbridge to Maidstone Bridge and return the next day with the exchanged pony. What a joyously care-free occupation!

I recall having a lesson in ploughing with the old Kent reversible plough, teamed by a most unlikely pair of horses. It happened this way. Our farm on what is now the Ridgewaye was prepared to receive almost anything in the way of food for pigs. Everything was cooked in an enormous boiler.

One day a knacker's cart arrived with a horse condemned and declared useless by the vet as suffering from paralysis. It was accepted on the understanding that Dick, our cowman, would use the newly invented humane pistol and that the meat would be used as pig food.

Dick, who was notably clever with animals, pleaded with my father to be allowed to prove the vet wrong. Reluctantly my father, who was a JP, technically broke the law and allowed him to put the mare in a spare cow-stall as a sick-bay. She was up and about in three weeks and soon ready to do a day's work – hence the odd-looking pair in the plough ropes. Five shillings was the price paid to the dead-meat man, the knacker, and so she had to be named 'The Dollar Princess'.

A favourite with the family was 'Bob', a rather wild, loveable little pickle of a forest pony. In those days it was not uncommon to see a couple of drovers with a string of ten or twelve forest ponies, half-broken, travelling through the towns and villages selling them off as they went.

Bob served well for many years but once, while being watered at the horse-trough by Skinners' School, he was maliciously flicked with a whip by a stupid carter. Bob bolted right through St John's and arrived driverless in Southborough.

Every time he passed the same spot, he would try to bolt. I did not know this and he played the same game with me. We zig-zagged along the main road (imagine it now

A delivery cart belonging to G.E. Farrant, haulage contractor, early twentieth century. The man is George Waghorn and he is standing on North Farm Road, outside the Royal Kent Laundry.

in today's traffic) right through Southborough and he only answered the bit when we reached the Common. He then turned and trotted home.

I have one curious memento which I keep with other odds and ends in my little workshop. It is an ash pole covered in leather, about eight feet long; it was the spread pole used when two ponies were harnessed to the family wagonette. We sat sideways on long seats. My job was to take out the enormous canvas umbrella from a long wicker basket to protect the ladies if a shower threatened.

The local lads had an astonishingly efficient grape-vine for information. News would quickly spread when a notorious mule, 'Charlie Chaplin', formerly belonging to the Army, was to be shod.

He was a huge beast and could only be managed by three men. After throwing the poor creature, one man would sit on his head, another on his rump, whilst the farrier did his best to re-plate him. We boys always secretly hoped that one or all of the men would be maimed for life – we were certainly on the side of the mule.

Another example of the grape-vine intelligence was when word went round 'they are going to do a wheel'. This also involved the forge and entailed a wonderful piece of timing between Bill Carter, the farrier, his mate and the wheelwright. The great wooden wagon wheel was trundled into the yard, hub, spokes and felloe (the exterior rim of the wheel) duly assembled over a stone depression where it could be spun on an iron spike in the centre.

The 5th Southborough Guides, c. 1915. From left to right, back row: ? Walker, -?-, -?-, Dorothy Barry, Katherine Wickenden, Violet Young (?). Front row: Hilda Page, Kathleen Cox (later married George Paine), Emily Waters (?), Alice Lewis, May Burr.

Meanwhile, inside the forge, the smith's mate was slowly turning the great iron tyre in the furnace, heating it section by section until the whole beautiful circle was glowing cherry-red. Now came the moment of drama. Two men, armed with huge tongs, carried the incandescent halo out to the yard. To a devil-dance by the three men, dimly seen through clouds of smoke and steam, wood and iron were wedded.

Consummation of the marriage was soon quenched by buckets of most unholy water drawn from the yard pump. Primitive but scientific. The shrinking tyre was clamping the joints of the wheel irrevocably and at the same time the metal was case-hardening.

A wiping of sweating brows on shirt sleeve and apron, and a quasi-severe admonition: 'now you boys, get along home now', indicated that the show was over. Another wheel was ready to roll.

The hay-loft over the main stable was usually a grand place to play. Trusses of hay could be made into a mystery cave or a desperately defended fortress. Once, however, the hay loft became a sanctuary for a lad too proud to weep in public yet distressed beyond measure from the events of the previous hour.

The Army in 1914 still considered the horse to be essential for transport when making war and, like other stables, we had to submit to our quota of horses being requisitioned. We lost three, naturally the best, and I can even now recall the indignity of that branding iron carried by a trooper from the forge, and again sense the smell of burning hair. No money could compensate for that feeling of loss.

Nobby Clark was our most popular roundsman. His horse's coat always shone the brightest, the hooves were blackened, the harness and brass the most highly polished, the van well washed and the wheels well greased.

We boys loved Nobby. His hair-raising tales – probably quite untrue – of adventure whilst driving the four-in-hand coach to Speldhurst and beyond would delight us but, best of all, he would sometimes hand us the reins and teach us horse-sense.

It was a sad disillusion when, in later years, Nobby was to be seen trying to drive a Ford van. He could never be broken of the habit of jerking the steering-wheel when chugging up a long hill, as if encouraging a weary pony.

In later life, George Paine was a successful headmaster of a school in Erith; he married Miss Kathleen Cox, a teacher at St Peter's School on the Common and a local Girl Guide leader. When George's father, the director of the bakery Paine, Smith, died in 1942, the Kent Education Committee wanted George to stay in teaching but realized that someone had to run what was a vital element in food production, providing bread to a district with many evacuees. He was often asked how the change from schoolmaster to baker affected him and he told the Kent & Sussex Courier *in 1988: 'It's simple. There is little difference between running a school and a business. In the business I had a staff of over fifty and many of them were exactly like children in many ways. There were four shops, nine rounds and a flourishing wholesale connection. Plant and machinery in the two bake houses were adequate but much outdated and our fleet, if you could call them that, of eleven vans were difficult to maintain as new plant and vans were virtually unobtainable.' George died in 1998.*

Southborough in the '20s

Clement Pain moved from Leatherhead to Fairlawn, 4 Park Road (now demolished and replaced by flats for the elderly) in May 1919. He has some Southborough memories of the 1920s.

J. Martin and Sons of London Road moved us. One of the three vans was a steam wagon. My father, one of the four doctors in Southborough, owned one of the very few cars in the town, a Mass, a green two-seater with a 'dickey'. This was succeeded in 1924 by a Bean, also a two-seater, maximum speed 35mph. There were no petrol pumps in Southborough, and I well remember Mr Webb, the owner of the Central Garage, next to the Weavers, delivering in a handcart twelve two-gallon tins of petrol, to be stored at the back of our garage.

Buses from Tunbridge Wells, run by the Autocar Bus Company, went no further than the Fountain. Quarry Hill into Tonbridge was considered too steep. However, sometime in the early '20s, the Redcar Company began to operate in competition; by then they all went as far as Tonbridge station. A price war ensued. 'A penny all the way,' shouted the rival conductors at Tunbridge Wells station. Then followed an exciting race as Redcar tried to overtake Autocar, to pick up more passengers at the next stop, to be crammed into an already overfull bus.

Tuesday was market day at Tonbridge. No cattle transporters then – all the cattle and sheep were driven through Southborough by the drovers. Woe betide those who forgot to close their front gates.

The shops along the Parade were all different then. Hitch the ironmonger; Killick the dairy, who delivered milk in an

London Road, Southborough, shortly before the First World War.

Hackett's the butchers with delivery cart, at the corner of Still Lane and London Road.

open-ended pony trap, with two twenty-gallon churns; Damper the second-hand junk shop; Mrs Savill who had a small greengrocer's at the corner of Castle Street; Langford the baker; Burchett the fishmonger – he was a keen cricketer for Southborough; Fielder, Jarret and Ransome, three elderly ladies who ran a stationer's-cum-newsagent but never had anything you wanted! There was Green's the chemist – I have a book given to my father by Mr Green in memory of his son who was killed riding his bicycle along the main road near the shop. Then came Fielder the grocer; Wratten at the post office, where sweets were sold; and opposite, at the corner of Holden Road, Hackett the butcher.

Frank Woolley, the Test cricketer, lived in Yew Tree Road and was, at least in the eyes of one young schoolboy, Southborough's most illustrious resident. His presence in the back pew at St Peter's church compensated for having to sit through the seemingly interminable service, usually lasting one and three-quarter hours.

Southborough in those days was a town proud of its own identity. It was separated from Tunbridge Wells by half a mile of open fields, along what was called the Lew.

Fred Ongley

Frederick H. Ongley was born in Southborough in 1918 and lived in Taylor Street until 19 December 1939 when he enlisted in the RAF. He was taken prisoner-of-war in Java by the Japanese and did not return home until October 1945. A few weeks later he married the fiancée he had left behind and they moved to Rusthall.

I remember standing in for a friend, who had broken a leg whilst learning to ride a bicycle, and working on Saturday mornings at Paine, Smith's on the corner of Speldhurst Road and London Road, and in the afternoons at their other shop in Holden Park Road. My job was to deliver cakes to Wratten's post office on the Parade, and elsewhere. Later I started work at B.W. Poile, electrical engineer, radio and television, where Bill Howes, father of John Howes, was my 'understudy'.

I remember large gates at both ends of Broomhill Park Road, with only swing gates for pedestrians to pass through. At that time, the land belonged to the Salomons Estate and the UDC was reluctant to take it over.

In those days, before the war, Penticost's cows used to graze on the Common and Huckleberry Wood, now Whortleberry Wood, was all fenced in and strictly out of bounds to us boys. The gravel pit had slides down the sides which were lubricated by boys standing at the top. And there was a football ground behind Prospect Road.

There was an annual parade in memory of those who lost their lives on the troopship HMS *Hythe* in 1915 near Gallipoli. I was a member of the Scout band and we used to lead the parade from Western Road to St Peter's church. Two of us used to sound *The Last Post* at the War Memorial. At the Silver Jubilee celebrations for King George V [1935], almost every shop in Southborough had festoons of coloured lights and decorative crowns, with a celebration archway across London Road by the Royal Victoria Hall.

Behind the Bell Inn, there was an open-air swimming pool which was used as an emergency water supply during the war. Sometimes there was dancing on the cricket pitch in the evenings, to records amplified from a pantechnicon provided by Martins Removals Ltd.

There were two forges in Southborough

The Bell Inn, Southborough. This building was demolished in March 2000.

back then, one in Forge Road and one in Holden Road. I remember the installation of probably the first television set in Southborough, at Sinden's, the butcher, in Holden Park Road. The dramatist Christopher Fry, who wrote *A Phoenix Too Frequent* and *The Lady's Not For Burning* amongst other plays, was director of the Tunbridge Wells Repertory Players between 1932 and 1935; he lived at Rough Down, opposite the present Q8 petrol station.

And finally, I remember going off to war, but I will always remember the wonderful 'Welcome Home' which the people of Taylor Street gave me on my return in October 1945, with the whole road filled with flags and bunting – a much-treasured memory of Southborough.

Growing up in the '30s

Mrs Yvonne V. Hanmore remembers her time growing up in Southborough before the Second World War. She now lives in Eastbourne.

I came to live in Sussex with my husband in 1946, when he was demobbed from the RAF, but my mother continued to live in Southborough until her death in 1974, so we still came often to visit with the children.

We moved to Holden Park Road about 1927 and lived right by Paine, Smith's bakery yard, where the horse drawn carts were kept. My brother and I would watch the great horses being taken out of the shafts and led through the yard to their stables beyond, by the alley-way which linked Prospect Road to London Road. From the yard we could walk through to the forge and watch the blacksmith at work shoeing the horses – hands over our ears to shut out the noise. How black everything was, but we could also walk right through the bakehouse where everything was white and the men were covered with flour. The bread and cakes were really first class. I remember especially the big round Coburg loaves, with the top crust split in a cross, so that we could each have a corner pulled off, and what a crust!

There was another, less pleasant, odour which only occasionally made itself known to us as we walked through the tanyard on the way to the Common. Perhaps there was some connection with the slaughter-house behind Hill's, the butcher, on London Road. That was a scary place for me, when the cattle truck backed up to the big gate and the animals were let down into the yard,

bellowing and clumping in protest.

I first went to school at the Brightridge primary school in Charles Street. The headmistress was Miss Wells, and I think there was only one other teacher, Miss Presnall. The building does not seem to have changed externally, though the iron railings which used to enclose the playground were taken away in the war, to be melted down for munitions.

When I was eight I went to the 'big school' on the Common. It would have been about a one-mile walk each way, so I took my lunch in a little brown attaché-case; cold beef sandwiches always remind me of that. Each child was given a small bottle of milk, a third of a pint, for lunch. In winter, the cream on top froze and pushed off the little cardboard lid, but it tasted wonderful.

In summer there were huge buttercups in the cow-meadow below the cricket pitch. If you lay down, carefully, among them, you were almost hidden. We had many picnics

The Royal Victoria Hall before the façade was changed in 1977. The photograph was actually taken in 1910.

there and on the cricket pitch, under the two great oaks, where the new mown grass used to be piled up, just right for us to play in.

As children, the Common seemed such a marvellous place for adventures, it had so many little paths to explore, shady secret places for picnics, huge trees for hide-and-seek, and some for climbing if you were brave enough. We loved walking to the Beehive at Modest Corner for a treat – a glass of lemonade and a packet of biscuits on the grass among the buttercups. Inside the Beehive there would hardly have been enough room for a dozen people, I think, it

was so small. Sometimes on our walks, we would take a basket or two and fill them with sticks and pine cones for our fires, or with leaf-mould for the garden. I am not sure if those things are permitted now.

Coming home, via London Road, I remember the front of the Royal Victoria Hall as it was, the red plush tilting seats, children's films on Saturday mornings, my first long-dress dance, many, many jumble sales, Christmas parties, etc.

Opposite the 'Vic' was a corn and seed merchant – Pollington? – and behind their shop, in Bedford Road, was a coal merchant's yard, where we could watch the coal being weighed on enormous scales and put into sacks. People could bring little carts and buy what they needed – or could afford.

I love St Peter's church, for that is where my husband and I were married. I remember we had to go to Modest Corner to the verger to arrange for the ceremony, which was conducted by Reverend Hanbury Head.

During the war, I worked in a Government office in Tunbridge Wells and cannot remember much of what Southborough was like then, except, for some reason, the number of the town fire station in London Road – Station 31 CIV.

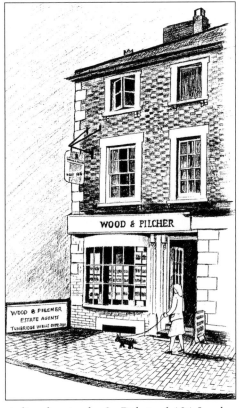

A line drawing by S. Bishop of 124 London Road today. It used to be Marshall's the butchers.

Butchers and Fishmongers

Mrs N. Goodland remembers her family's meat and fish businesses.

My grandfather used to have a butcher's shop in what is now Wood & Pilcher, the estate agent on the corner of Holden Park Road and London Road. Back in the last decade of the nineteenth century, Reginald Marshall moved his butcher's shop from Speldhurst to Southborough. Grandfather used to buy the cattle in Tonbridge market and they were driven along the road to be slaughtered in the abattoir behind what is now the Hospice in the Weald shop and the hairdressers in London Road. This was rented from a Mr Dickinson, also a butcher in Tunbridge Wells. There are still folk in Southborough who remember seeing the little calves being carried into the abattoir.

The horse and cart used to make the meat deliveries from the shop. They were stabled in Holden Park Road, just opposite the present Sugar City shop, and at weekends Jack, the horse, grazed in a field where now stand the Gallard almshouses.

The chickens sold in the shop were kept in a field where the library now stands and at Christmas time they were held in what was the laundry in Bedford Road before they were killed for the table.

'Pincher' Sinden, who had a butcher's shop at the top of Charles Street, learned his trade from my grandfather in the London Road shop, which closed soon after the First World War because my grandfather would not sell imported meat, and he retired.

My father went into the fish trade, and had the first fish and chip shop in Southborough. It was in Western Road, opposite the Men's Club, in the hut later occupied by John Moon the cobbler, until it was pulled down in 1999. During the day my father did a fish round in the country areas. He had two cousins – Evan, who had a fish shop at the Yew Tree Road end of Southborough, and Sid, who had a fish shop opposite the Bell Inn before it was demolished in 2000. Sid also ran a country 'round'.

My father was killed in 1926, in a motorcycle accident, but the other Marshall 'boys' carried on in the fish business until after the Second World War.

John Moon repaired shoes for twenty-four years in his tiny cobbler's shop in Western Road. On retirement in 1999 his shop, complete with tools and contents, moved to the Museum of Kent Life at Cobtree, Maidstone. (Courier photograph)

The Fever Hospital

Mr and Mrs Lawrence were appointed to the posts of superintendent and matron of the Fever Hospital in Vauxhall Lane in April 1911. They were married in Capel church, as they both worked in the village hospital there, but they moved to Southborough to take up their new jobs on the same day that they became husband and wife. Their daughter, now Mrs Joan

The Superintendent's house at the Fever Hospital in Vauxhall Lane. This is now Moatenden.

The mortuary of the Vauxhall Lane Fever Hospital.

Branch, was born in the house in the hospital grounds (it is now called Moatenden) and she and her two siblings lived there until it closed in 1939.

None of us three were ever patients. Carbolic soap, Jeyes Fluid and much scrubbing overcame any chance of infection from the wards and clothing was always changed by those working with the in-patients. We were never kissed although we were lovingly cared for.

There was usually a regular supply of patients and sometimes an epidemic. Extra nurses were then called from London, or from Mrs Mannering's Nursing Agency in Park Road. My mother always went with my father in the horse-drawn ambulance to collect the patients. Father, as superintendent, would seal the house and bring the bedding to the hospital for fumigation. Patients were mostly children with diphtheria, scarlet fever and typhoid. Visitors were allowed twice a week. They rang the bell at the gate and were able to communicate through a curtained observation window. Any toys brought to the hospital had to be left there.

There were two brick built wards for diphtheria and scarlet fever and, sadly, a mortuary. Duration of stay was usually a month for diphtheria and six weeks for scarlet fever.

Mother would nurse night and day if necessary, tending the patients as if they were her own family. Christmas Day was celebrated for the patients; Boxing Day was for us children. Staff included a resident cook and ward maid, with a laundress who came three times a week. The laundress used copper boilers, with a coal-fired ironing and airing room. The irons were heated on the stove. There was no gas or electricity, although there was a telephone. All the wards had coal fires and cooking was on a coal range, which also heated the water. The hospital and house were lighted by oil lamps and candles.

In the event of an epidemic, the veranda was boarded up to make another ward. The nurses slept in the house in times of emergency. The house had four bedrooms, a bathroom and toilet upstairs with two large rooms (a dining/doctor's room and sitting room) downstairs. There was also a kitchen, scullery, pantry and a store room.

The large garden supplied vegetables and my father was the gardener and he sometimes had some help. The lawn and banks were thick with daffodils, fir trees were planted to line the drive, and wild flowers grew in profusion.

Father, sadly, succumbed to 'flu in 1932; he was forty-nine years old. Mother remained at the hospital until her retirement which coincided with the closure in October 1939. She moved to Reynolds Lane and died in 1951, aged seventy-four.

There were no lights in Vauxhall Lane when I lived there – the family, the staff, postman, tradespeople – all walked down and up the hilly lane at all times and in all weathers.

Marjorie Stent

As a young girl and teenager Marjorie Elliot lived in a stone cottage at 108 Edward Street. Her father, Charlie, was a survivor of the HMS Hythe disaster in 1915. The ship was sunk accidentally by another British ship as they tried to land troops in the Dardanelles. Of the 433 men on HMS Hythe, 350 drowned, including Captain David Salomons, the son and heir to Broomhill Park, and many

RANK	NAME
CAPTAIN	D. REGINALD SALOMONS
C.S.M.	CARTER, JOHN HENRY
SERGEANT	FULLER, WILLIAM BROOKES
,,	READER, FRANK ARTHUR
CORPORAL	GROOMBRIDGE, WILLIAM
,,	SOMERS, FREDERICK
II ,,	FARNES, ROBERT
II ,,	HAWKINS, CLEMENT
II	HEAD, ALBERT

Part of the memorial in St Matthew's church, High Brooms, to those who drowned when HMS Hythe sank on 28 October 1915.

local men. Charlie was pulled exhausted from the sea and after he had recovered was sent to fight at the Front in France. During one action he had his foot shot off and gangrene set in and his leg had to be amputated. After the war, he earned his living and supported his wife and five children by stitching cricket balls for Wisden's in his garden shed. His war pension helped – it amounted to £1 0s 4d a week. Marjorie is now Mrs Stent and remembers Southborough in the 1920s and 1930s.

Cattle used to be driven along London Road to the slaughterhouse which was behind the butcher's shop near the Flying Dutchman Inn. Nurse Harvey was the local midwife. She was a big lady in a navy blue uniform, who rode a three-wheeler cycle. Whenever we saw the three-wheeler outside a house, we knew there would be a new baby but, as kids, we never knew where she got the baby from!

Mr Davis was the postman. He wore a hat with a piece at the front and the back so that the rain ran off. He always knocked the door-knocker to let you know that he had put a letter through the letter-box.

Reverend Russell Howden (vicar from 1917 to 1938) preached at St Peter's church. I always thought he was Jesus, as he looked like him, with a beard. We lived by the sound of St Peter's bells, telling us when to be in school, and dinner time, and when to go home. On May Day we had a maypole on a piece of the green in front of St Peter's church. Mr Burr was the local policeman – woe betide any boy caught kicking a football in the street.

Mr Penticost was the milkman from

Bentham Farm in Modest Corner. He came round with a yoke on his shoulders and two large cans of milk, from which he ladled out whatever you wanted, usually a half-pint, but he came round early in the morning and again in the late afternoon.

Mr Neal used to live in a house just past the Royal Victoria Hall. He would charge battery accumulators for sixpence. You had to leave them with him for a week, and then you could listen to the wireless.

Two single-decker buses used to run through Southborough along London Road. They were Redcar and Autocar. They used to race to get in front of each other, to pick up the passengers first.

Mules', the bakers, was on the corner of Speldhurst Road and London Road. On Monday mornings, they sold off all the stale cakes from the previous week; you got a shopping bag full, with a cream one on the top, for threepence or a smaller bag for twopence.

Hythe Sunday was commemorated on the nearest Sunday to the date of the disaster, 28 October. The survivors used to march behind a band to St Peter's church, after a reunion dinner the previous evening at the drill hall in Speldhurst Road.

Sir David Salomons was one of the first men to own a motor car, and my mother remembered seeing a man walking in front of it waving a red flag. She also remembered seeing the family riding in a horse-drawn sleigh when it snowed. He

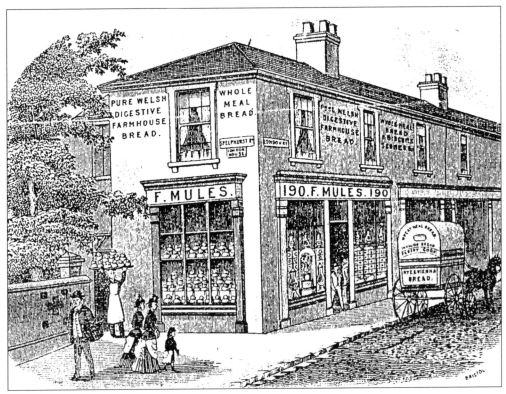

F. Mules' bakery at 190 London Road, in an engraving taken from their invoice head, 1895.

34

The staff of the International Stores in London Road outside their shop, c. 1910. (Courier photograph)

owned beautiful horses and it was said that when any of his horses were ill, he would order a bottle of whisky for them.

The School Board man would ride around Southborough, looking all over for kids who were not at school. The lamplighter would also ride around on his bicycle just before dark, with a short ladder over his shoulder, to light the gas lamps in the street. Mr Bond, the greengrocer, would deliver even in the dark with a candle in a lamp on either side of his horse and cart. The International Stores was at 72 London Road. At Christmas one year I remember they sold forty oranges for one shilling. Finally, I remember Freddy Legget, known as the 'Toy Drum Major'. He played a toy drum and you could hear him coming from a long way off. People did say that he was shell-shocked during the First World War.

The Clay Pit

Miss Janet Hancock used to live in High Brooms in the 1940s and often used to play in the clay pit that serviced the brickworks.

As kids we were always over the clay pit even though we were not supposed to play there as it was dangerous with all the trolleys and machinery. After the clay was dug it was put into trolleys which were pulled up the slope to the brickworks by fixed rope. A klaxon used to sound when they were about to be sent back down the slope to warn people. These trucks made an enormous rattling noise as gravity took them back down again. Kitty Hicks, the daughter of the works manager, and I were friends and their house had a finial on its roof of an angel. This was blown down and smashed in the great storm of 1987.

Unloading trolleys of clay at High Brooms brickworks.

Presentation of the 'Clay Industries Award' at the High Brooms Brick & Tile Co. Ltd. Those in the foreground are, from left to right, Len Vidler, Ted Simmons (recipient of the award), Gerald Weare (co-owner of the brickworks), Tom Edwards (works manager).

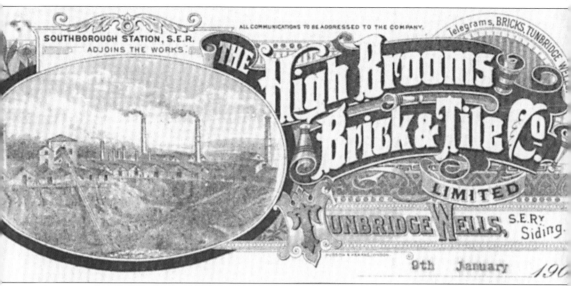

Letterhead of the High Brooms Brick & Tile Co., 1907.

Bill Aldred

Bill Aldred was one of nine brothers and sisters who were born and brought up in High Brooms. (See photographs overleaf)

We all went to school in High Brooms, either the Boys' or the Girls' School. My dad, Len, went to the Boys' School too; in fact, I have a medal of his that he was awarded 'for perfect attendance and good conduct' from 1908 to 1913. He was chairman of High Brooms Working Men's Club for twenty-five years before he died in 1982, at the age of eighty-two.

I left school quite early. My mum said I was worth more out in the fields fruit picking! I remember Jesse Hollamby used to have a Sunday afternoon second-hand furniture sale on his plot of land, where he kept chickens and pigs, on the corner of Powdermill Lane and Brokes Way. You could get a big jug for 2s 6d; these were very popular in High Brooms because most of us

were born in our own homes and you needed plenty of hot water.

High Brooms Ancestors

Mary Blake, who lives at 21 Highfield Road, has researched her family history and discovered that its association with High Brooms goes back four generations. Her great-grandfather, James Scrace, was born in Street in Sussex on 2 June 1836 and her great grandmother was born Eliza Sayers in Shermanbury, Sussex a few years later.

The photo of James and Eliza (*see p. 39*) was taken in 1861 when they got married at Trinity Church, Hurstpierpoint, on 6 April, 1861. They walked four miles to the church, there and back, to get married. My great grandmother has a new dress and my great grandfather is wearing a new smock as he was a farm worker.

They came to live in High Brooms in July

Bill Aldred with his father's medal, awarded for perfect attendance and good conduct between 1908 and 1913 at High Brooms Boys' School.

Leonard Frederick Aldred's good conduct medal.

Eliza and James Scrace after their wedding, 6 April 1861.

Cows going to Northfield Farm pasture in Highfield Road, c. 1950.

1880 and my great-grandfather went to work for Mr Henry Reader at Home Farm, Colebrook Park. The following year he changed jobs and worked for Mr W.A. Smith at Colebrook Park and remained in the same service for him for twenty-five years.

In 1911 they celebrated their golden wedding anniversary at their home at 75 Colebrook Road and the *Advertiser* newspaper sent a reporter to interview them. At that time they had eight children living, twenty-three grand children and three great grandchildren.

James reminisced to the paper that he deplored the fact that he was not a scholar; he said that, when he was a child, he was often taken out of school when there was farm work to be done. 'People think times are hard now', he told the *Advertiser*, 'but they were harder then, when you had to make half an ounce of tea do for a week, and

when, if a man had twelve shillings a week and a house, he was well paid.'

When the couple first came to High Brooms there were not more than twenty houses in the district and all the land between Colebrook Road and the brickworks was dense woodland and trees grew where St Matthew's church is now. South View Road was a regular camping place for gipsies. My great grandmother remembered with evident amusement that the road through the woodland to the brickworks was so muddy that a friend of hers once lost a shoe and never did find it again!

One of James and Eliza's children, Sarah, had died in tragic circumstances in 1899. She was only twenty-seven and had married a brickworker named William Saunders and they had a child of fifteen months, my mother, Mary Eliza. They lived in 60 Colebrook Road. Grandmother was downstairs one evening with her husband and child asleep already upstairs. When the time came for her to go to bed, she went into the kitchen and bent over to blow out a paraffin lamp, a wedding present. As she did so it exploded and she was instantly enveloped in flames. Her night-dress burst into flames and she screamed out. Husband William ran down stairs to help her. He tried to put the flames out but couldn't and badly burned his hands.

Poor Grandmother was in such a frenzy that she ran outside and climbed over the fence into her neighbour's yard. The Haymans lived there and the son, Harry, jumped out the first floor back window and ran to help her and deftly enveloped her in a carpet to douse the flames. The inquest report tells that she was in such agony that she wrung her hands till the blood dripped from them and pieces of half burnt skin fell from her body onto the floor.

Mrs Hayman tried to treat the burns by pouring oil over them. Grandmother was delirious with pain and had to be restrained from running out into the street. Mr Hayman, in his pyjamas, ran to get a tradesman's cart to take her to hospital and Harry ran to the local police constable's house to raise the alarm. Soon the Jubilee ambulance arrived and took her to the hospital. She died of her injuries three days later without regaining consciousness. My mother didn't even wake up when all this was going on. Grandmother was pregnant at the time of the accident.

The Coroner recorded a verdict of 'accidental death' and agreed with the jury that the accident occurred because it was a cheap lamp and low grade American Tea Rose oil had been used in it. Vapour had built up in the well of the lamp and this had probably flashed when Grandmother blew it out. Harry Hayman was praised in particular for his courage at jumping from the first floor of his house to roll Grandmother up in the carpet and also for then putting out the fire in the kitchen.

My mother, Mary, married Gillham Henry Benton on 30 March 1918. He had fought in the war but had been gassed and lost a lung so was discharged from the Army. When he was well enough he drove a tram in London where he met my mother who was working at Woolwich Arsenal. After they married they returned to Tunbridge Wells and had a house in Queens Road where my sister Maggie and I were born. When I was fifteen in 1937 we moved to Nursery Road.

A year before moving to High Brooms I had joined the Tunbridge Wells Piano Accordion Band run by Frederick Charles Stanley Blake. When the Second World War came, Freddy was called up and was a warrant officer, ending up in radar before being demobbed. We married in October 1943 and at first lived with my parents in Nursery Road before getting the house in Highfield Road in 1948.

Freddy was very musical and interested in anything to do with electronics. He made two electronic organs, one of which had a special device which makes one voice sound like a choir, using 108 silicon chips. He could play them as well as the piano and piano accordion. His interest in electronics goes back to the time when he left King Charles School and became apprenticed as an electrical engineer. He was an avid reader of scientific journals and books and it was with the aid of these that he managed, at the age of twenty-two, to start selling do-it-yourself kits for the early televisions. That was in 1932 and he sold the sets for £2 10s. He got all the parts and showed people how to assemble the televisors which produced a pink picture. A local garage made the metalwork for him and his father cut out the wood. He also sold kits to a radio wholesaler but admitted that his business ventures never made much money. Freddy also made a special disc which could be played on a gramophone, which has been described as the world's first video recording at home.

In 1984 he took part in a *Pebble Mill at One* programme which marked the fifty years since television's inventor, John Logie Baird, terminated his contract with the BBC. Freddy was presented with a specially struck medal by the Royal Television Society. Only 160 of the medals were made and were donated by Radio Rentals, who bought the Baird trademark.

Our daughter Sue was born in 1951. For 20 years before Freddy's death in 1994, as a family we used to do charity work. We called ourselves 'The Jubilee Singers' and we used to dance, perform sketches as well as sing, anything from 1880 to the 1990s. We'd perform anywhere in Kent and Sussex – village and church halls, old peoples' homes, Old Time Music Hall shows in the Royal Victoria Hall, that sort of thing – and raised money for Cancer Research, Children In Need and the FRED Club which Daisy Fletcher set up in 1986 where disabled young people could socialize every Wednesday.

Wartime Wedding

Mrs Beryl Funnell (née Ashton) has lived at 23 Castle Street since 1945.

I first came to Southborough when I left school at fourteen and went into service for the Misses Readers, Dorothy and Ailee, who lived in a big house at the bottom of Pennington Road on the right. It was called Westwood but it has been pulled down now.

I remember my Mum saying to me: 'Right my lady, you're going to put your feet under somebody else's table now'. I had my own room and the spinsters, who came from a farming family around Yalding, paid me five shillings a week and I also got my meals free. The sisters were very good to work for. Sometimes they would let me and the chauffeur/gardener listen to the wireless in their sitting room. That's how I learned about the abdication of Edward VIII.

Most things were delivered in those days.

Vic Funnell (father of Alf) lived at 21 Castle Street and worked as a 'milkman's man' at Killick's Dairy.

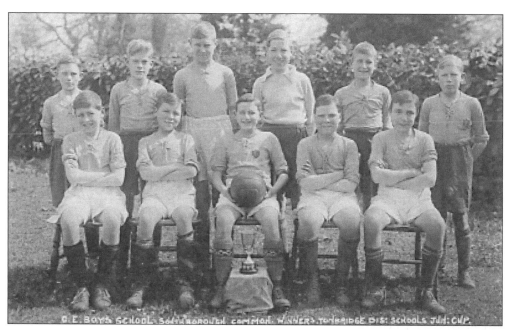

Southborough Church of England Boys' School football team between 1929 and 1932. They were winners of the Tonbridge District Schools Junior Cup. Alf Funnell is third from the left on the back row. The others are, from left to right, back row: Bernard Austin, Stan Keen, Alf Funnell, Jack Standing, Thomas Culmer, ? Chatfield. Front row: Des Botting, Fred Jeffrey, Harold Fletcher, Bill Rosewell, Frank Sutcliffe.

Greengroceries came from Lawrence's at the top of Pennington Road and were delivered by a young man called Alf. One day he did not appear so I asked another delivery man, Vic, who cycled up and down the road delivering milk from two cans hung on his handlebars, what had happened to Alf. The Readers got their milk twice daily from Killick's Dairy which is now the Lalipu Indian Restaurant. Vic said Alf had got a firework in his eye and would be off work for a bit. I didn't know that Alf was Vic's son!

Apparently Vic had gone home and said one of the maids in one of the big houses was asking after him, and that's how it all got started. The boys in Southborough would be courting the maids who worked in the houses in Pennington Road and,

because Westwood was right at the end, Alf used to collect all of them at the front gates at the end of the evening and they would all walk back up to Southborough together.

When the war started I was conscripted into the ATS – the Auxiliary Territorial Service – and Alf joined the Navy. I trained as a cook and was stationed with 486 Battery RA and then 546 Battery RA. We decided to get married and applied for a special licence – it cost ten shillings – and arrangements were made for Reverend Squire to do it at St Thomas's. Alf had got leave for twenty-one days and I had leave for fourteen.

We were due to marry on 30 April 1943 but the special licence did not arrive in the post that morning. Fortunately there were

Alf Funnell and Beryl Ashton were married on 30 April 1943. The photograph was taken by Stickles of Tunbridge Wells.

two posts in those days and it arrived in the second one at noon, and we were married at 3 p.m. I've still got my wedding dress – it cost £2 from Gees in Tunbridge Wells which was near the Cosmos cinema. We had to get Stickles in Tunbridge Wells to open up specially to take our wedding photo. The cake was from Paine, Smith, the baker, and looked very grand but it was mainly a cardboard cover over the cake itself – of course there was no icing sugar in those days.

During the war, we had fifteen days together out of four and a half years. Once I was with a battery in Anglesey in North Wales and Alf's ship HMS *Dido* was being repaired in Liverpool. I could see from the map that the two places were not very far apart so we applied for 48 hours' leave.

Everybody around where I was stationed spoke Welsh and I could not make myself understood when I went looking for two nights' bed and breakfast. Eventually one old lady said we could stay but only after I showed her the wedding photo to prove that we were married!

I was demobbed a month after the war was over – married women went first. We had been renting 23 Castle Street from Bill Sheepwash who had the garage at the end of the road – he ran a taxi business from it – and so we had somewhere to live. The rent was 15s a week.

We had utility furniture – we had enough dockets for a bed, sideboard, a table with four chairs and a small armchair. Alf was good at making things and made two bedside cabinets from wooden orange boxes which he varnished.

Alf went to work for Seeboard and I worked as a cleaner part time. In the Parade there was Mrs Pilcher, an outfitter, then next to that was Mrs Barker's sweet shop. It always smelt of paraffin when you went in there as there was a paraffin lamp out the back. I remember her breaking up nutty brittle with a small hammer. Next to her was Mr Grantham, the shoe repairer, and then Mr Nicols, the fishmonger, which before him used to be Mr Birchett, a greengrocer.

Alf's father Vic lived next door. His occupation on our wedding certificate was recorded as 'milkman's man'. Vic's father used to work at Stemp's Farm – now the Weavers. To earn some pocket money he would bundle up chopped wood to be used as kindling and sell them. These were called 'pimps'.

Everybody used to know everybody else in Castle Street and we were always popping in and out of each other's homes. It's not like that now. The last street party we had was for the Coronation in 1953.

Australia

Queenie Darvil of Stuart Cottage, London Road in Southborough is in her nineties and still going strong. She puts it down to sparkling wine: 'Champagne is a great uplifting force – I open a bottle everyday at the witching hour, noon.' If you visit her before the witching hour then you will be offered brandy and ginger wine with the traditional toast of 'Bung Ho!'. She got the habit of opening a bottle of bubbly everyday from her father, who did the same thing. He used to tell her: 'Yesterday is a cancelled cheque; tomorrow is a promissory note; today the only cash you have is in your hand so spend it well.' Every year she hosts four champagne mornings for Age Concern and the Lifeboats (RNLI).

My husband, Les, and I were married for fifty-six years. He was a corn merchant in Hadlow and was the only person I know who could walk round a field of corn and tell you exactly what weight it would thrash out. We moved here in the 1960s when Stuart Cottage was on offer for £19,000 – it was formerly three cottages that had been converted, rather badly, into one. Les bought it because the Greenline bus used to stop outside every half an hour and I used to have to go up to London in those days. King Charles I is supposed to have spent one night in the cellar of the cottage when he was on the run.

Although I was born in England, I went to Australia when I was three. By that time

Stuart Cottage, London Road, Southborough, today. Queenie Darvil is on the right.

Two views of Stuart Cottage, c. 1910. In the lower picture, the district nurse (left) and Mrs Elizabeth Wickenden are at the gate.

I could read fluently. I grew up on a sheep station where my father farmed 20,000 head of sheep and our nearest neighbour was 300 miles away. We used to love it when the sheep shearers arrived, as it was the only time there were enough people around for my father to have a game of cricket. At 4 p.m. each day the shearers would have their 'tea' – a combination of lunch, tea and supper – and I used to recite poems for them. Father was cricket mad and would arrange the cruet and cutlery in cricket positions on the dining room table before the supper was served. I came back to England when I was sixteen, although my family stayed in Australia.

In 1946, I went out to Australia again to sort out some family matters after my father died. I went on the *Stirling Castle* with the English cricket team under Wally Hammond. There were some great players and characters, the likes of Godfrey Evans, Len Hutton and Denis Compton – the Australian captain was Don Bradman. I watched every ball bowled in every Test match and in every other game they played as well. Not many people can say they have done that.

Holden House

Joyce Edna Cosham (née Stevenson) was born in 1920 in one of the estate cottages at Holden House as her father Sidney was the head gardener, of three. There were another eight domestic staff.

Next to our cottage was the stable yard. Although the mounting block was still there, the carriages had given way to cars, but the harness room was still more or less intact. However, the loose boxes and stalls housed lawn mowers, lawn sweepers and similar items.

The chauffeur lived in the other cottage. To the other side of our cottage was the laundry, with large copper and stone sink. It was no longer used, as the washing was sent out to a laundry in large wicker baskets. Leading from the laundry was the ironing room, again no longer used, but still with the cast iron stove with the shaped surfaces on which to heat the flat irons. Above the grass 'drying area' was the cart shed, then home to wheel barrows, hand barrows and miscellaneous items. Next door was the fruit room, housing the ripe fruit on slatted shelves, covered in hay, and root vegetables stored underneath in sand.

Behind the tool shed was the frame yard, leading to the potting shed and greenhouses. The three linking houses contained the vinery, tomato house and peach house. The plants that were to furnish the conservatory in the house were raised here and carried down, through the garden, on the hand barrow. The other greenhouse had figs, nectarines and a few orchids. The gardens were never short of water, for there were two springs in the top field, one of which flowed through the pleasure garden, starting in the gold fish pond, and the other one flowed into the frame yard supplying three water cress beds.

I think living in such an environment, I was introduced to fruit such as peaches, nectarines, grapes and figs, which my friends did not have. Admittedly, they were usually specimens that had dropped onto the staging and got bruised, so were not suitable for the 'big house'. From the vegetable garden came asparagus, globe artichoke and sea kale. There was also a nut walk and a walnut tree, but the squirrels did not leave many.

Hartridge Brothers butchers in the early twentieth century. The shop was founded in 1904 and was still trading in 1969; it is now Southborough Butchers. The butchers in the doorway are Baden (left) and Frank Hartridge.

We had one horse, Peggy, retired after the First World War but still needed, very grudgingly, to do a little work occasionally. This was usually rolling the drive or the grass tennis court; for that she had to wear leather shoes strapped to her hooves.

In those days, most tradesmen delivered. The baker, Paine, Smith, came every day with a horse and van, carrying the bread in large wicker baskets. Charlie, the butcher boy, called two or three times a week for orders and delivered them later in the morning, by bike of course. Similarly the grocer on a Friday and the 'Oil Man' with paraffin on a Friday afternoon. All the errand boys whistled! The milkman,

Penticost, delivered twice a day, the milk being measured by the pint and half-pint measures carried inside the large can. Our milkman had the right to graze his cattle on the Common and they would wander down to drink at Holden Pond before going back to Modest Corner and their farm. There were postal deliveries and collections three times a day.

At the top of Holden Road was the smithy, still very much in use then as there were a lot of horses still on the roads. We loved to gather round the doorway, for we were not allowed inside, to watch in the rather murky atmosphere, and the smell when the hot shoe was put on the hoof cannot be described or forgotten.

There were two laundries at Modest Corner – the Yew Tree Hand Laundry and Hill View Laundry on Victoria Road which was a machine laundry. This one dried the sheets on lines on its roof, while the hand laundry had a drying ground on the Common. The works hooter was blown at five minutes to the hour and on the hour at 8 a.m., 1 p.m., 2 p.m. and 5 p.m., a very useful timekeeper.

We used to play over the Common. There used to be slides down the gravel pit which were lubricated with frog spawn in the spring. I kept away from the boggy end, but what a lovely playground it was!

In one small area of the 'Pineys' in spring, there was a little patch of wood anemones, the only one I knew on the Common. At the back of Chapman's Green, by the side of the footpath from the Fountain to the Tanyard, was a small scattered patch of harebells. These were in addition to all the usual flowers: the heather, the milkwort, whortleberry, etc. And in the autumn there was a great assortment of fungi.

There was a sort of allotment, surrounded by a thick holly hedge on the edge of the Common, just behind the Yew Tree Hand Laundry at Modest Corner. It was cultivated by Mr Oyler, who lived in the house just above St Peter's church, known as 'Cats Castle'.

And is the 'Horse Ring' still there, near Modest Corner? It was a completely grass covered area, in the middle of the trees, a wonderful playground. I remember going there as a Girl Guide, for tracking, etc. I also

Holden House.

remember Mr Cullen, an auxiliary postman, who beat carpets over there. He came from Meadow Road and would push the carpets on an old pram to the Horse Ring, and when they had had a thorough beating he would push them back to their owners. When the wind was in the right direction, we could hear him beating them from our home at Holden House.

And what of the Annual Sports Evening on the Common, around the cricket pitch? Races for all ages, relay races, tug-of-war, but the real highlight of the evening was the cycle races. Our local favourite champion was Bob Laurence. 'Go it Bob!' we all screamed. I think he came from Hawkenbury.

Another annual fixture was the 'Top Hat Cricket Match'. I can still see some of the players, Mr Whibley, the jeweller, Mr Burchett, greengrocery and fish, Mr Hartridge, the butcher, who I think was an umpire. I used to have a record of these matches on postcards, but they were lent out and never returned. A great pity.

I remember Holden Pond being frozen solid enough for a few skaters to perform, while we children had two long slides, one coming and one going across the pond. I also recall getting 'bootsful' as the ice began to break up around the edges. And how about the enormous quantity of baby frogs, hopping about in all directions from the pond, after the spawn had developed into tadpoles, then frogs? There used to be a few strings of toad spawn in the pond, but I don't ever remember seeing a baby toad. The pond was also the scene of the Fire Brigade's wet drill. I can still remember Fireman 'Fatty' Kettle driving the engine and Fireman Bert Miles, but the other names I have forgotten.

The Common was a wonderful playground for us all – we built camps, buried treasures, then dug them up again, played 'houses' among the large roots of some trees. In fact, it was a happy, carefree safe time and I greatly regret that those times are over.

Reg Strutt

Reg Strutt was born in Nursery Road, High Brooms on 25 June 1911 and, except for a few months when his father's work took the family to London, he has lived in the town all his life. Reg was on the High Brooms Old Boys' Football Club committee for fifty years.

My first recollection is watching my father breaking up a block of ice to make ice cream to sell in the shop we had in 48 High Brooms Road. Other sweets were in big sweet jars and we used to break the lemonade bottles to get the marbles from the necks. I remember my father going off to war in 1916. I still have a Christmas card he sent to me. My mother worked in the Woodlands Laundry in Upper Grosvenor Road. Food was scarce in those days – often dinner was mashed potatoes with bread and lard. We had to go to Paine, Smith in Southborough and queue for the bread.

I went with my aunty to the nursery in High Brooms Road to pick heads off marigolds. They were used to make medicine for the war effort and we were paid one penny for a basket full. I used to go looking for my older brother and he always had to take me back home after I found him at the school. I did this so many times that eventually I was allowed to stay.

After the war we moved to Camberwell where my grand-dad Alfred had a barber's shop and my father used to cut the hair and

High Brooms Working Men's Club quoits team, winners of the Tonbridge and District Quoits League in 1921. There used to be a quoits pitch where no. 100 High Brooms Road now stands. From left to right, back row: George H. Moore, Ernest Pronger, William Bridges, H. 'Patsy' Smith, Arthur Morley, Ernest Turk. Front row: S. Moore, Dennis Hawkins, Charlie Hawkins, Alfred Parker.

shave customers. He got fed up when one of the other workers in the shop used to leave a customer half-shaved to go over the road to the pub! After six months my father lathered up one customer and said he was leaving and walked out. We came back to 48 High Brooms Road but my father was out of work. Because he had no money for the gas, he built an oven up against the back wall of the house with bricks and clay and my brother and I used to collect sticks to keep the fire going. Dad kept sixty chickens behind 48 High Brooms Road and fed them greenstuff from his allotment. He kept them for the eggs which he sold.

Dad let the shop to John Carter who used to do boot and shoe repairs and when I was eleven I used to help in the shop after

school, taking off the old soles, rasping around the new edges then polishing them and delivering them to the customers.

My mother used to help make ends meet by taking in washing. Dad made me a trolley and every Monday I had to walk to the Grove on the other side of Tunbridge Wells and pick up the washing from a family who lived there. I had to be at school before nine and if I was late I was caned on the hand. Kids don't know they're born today! We had a coal-fired copper in the scullery for this washing and every Friday I would take the clean clothes back in the trolley. I used to get a penny every Saturday for this – you could do what you like with it then.

I remember going with a basin to the butcher's on Fridays for pease pudding and

An outing to Margate from the Bat and Ball Inn, Southborough, September 1947.

faggots – there were seven different butchers in High Brooms then. For a penny you could also get a basin of pickled cabbage or onions.

There used to be a clay quoit pitching area next to the High Brooms Hotel. The iron quoits weighed 7lb. A man called Easterfield had the foundry beyond the brick works. You can still see his name on the manhole covers in the town. He took us boys for Bible study in the Wesleyan Chapel. I can feel the pain now – if you moved around he would grab your knees with his horny old hands to make you sit still!

When I was older, a friend and I used to go on a motorbike and side car to Camber Sands for a day out. Sam Lambert used to live in Horsmonden and he would pick me up. Once in 1931 we borrowed swimming costumes and took some of my father's home made cider and went to Camber. I must have fallen asleep in the sun and got really

burned. I was in bed for a week after that. My bedroom was full of bloody confetti when the skin peeled off!

I started work as a mechanic for BP who had a lorry garaged at the West Station goods yard. I then worked for Autocar which was run by a Welsh bloke who used to sack his drivers and, when he saw them standing around the town, he would tell them to hurry up and get back to work! I finished up working for Maidstone and District, and was there for forty-eight years.

High Brooms Shops and Services

George Corbett now lives in Prospect Road, Southborough but he was born in High Brooms in 1908 and lived there for the next thirty years. He remembers the people and businesses back when he was growing up before the Second World War.

High Brooms was almost a self-contained community, with its church and vicar, Philip Orme, and two chapels, Wesleyan and Bethel. It had two schools, one for infants and boys and one for girls. The infants were mixed boys and girls (three to seven years old) and the boys were seven to fourteen years old, under Mr Malpass the headmaster, assisted by Mr Livsey and Mr Wilsdon. In 1914, Messrs Livsey and Wilsdon were called up to serve in the Army and were replaced by a retired master, a Mr Diggens, a real tyrant, and a Miss Baker. The girls' school was in Great Brooms Road under Miss Austen, headmistress.

The area was under the control of the Southborough Urban District Council, which was the rating authority and was responsible for the maintenance of the roads and pavements and for refuse collection and disposal. We had our own road sweeper, and the roads and pavements were immaculate, unlike today.

The lighting was by gas light, with gas supplied by Tunbridge Wells Gas Company, maintained by the Council. We had our own police constable, PC Castle, who lived in High Brooms Road. One thing we did not have was a doctor in residence. You had to go to the surgery in London Road or Park Road, Southborough.

For recreation for the grown-ups there was the High Brooms Hotel and the Working Men's Club, and for the teenagers there was the Church Army at St Matthew's Parish Hall, run by Captain Smith and later on by Captain Williams. We played billiards, darts, shove ha'penny and cards and we were able to buy light refreshments. We also had a football team and competed in the Speldhurst and District League.

The demolition of High Brooms Girls' School, 1991.

High Brooms station, c. 1910.

Employment in the area was very good. High Brooms Brick and Tile Company was the main employer, along with the Tunbridge Wells Gas Company. For the females there was the Royal Kent Laundry, the Woodlands Laundry, many other small laundries and also the Photochrom Company in Upper Grosvenor Road, which produced greetings cards, postcards etc.

Housing was no problem. There was always an empty property somewhere. There were no council houses and few people owned their own house and, in the main, they rented. The brick company was the main landlord and it built and owned quite a lot of High Brooms. Rents were moderate and included rates (5s) and water rate (7s 6d) for a three-bedroomed house.

Transport out of High Brooms was by railway from Southborough station; later it was renamed High Brooms. Bus services started in the early 1920s; the buses ran from the railway station to Tunbridge Wells station. Oscar Pritchard operated the Autocar service and these were joined later by Redcar.

South View Road was divided into two. One side was in Tunbridge Wells and the other side in High Brooms. At the top was St Matthew's vicarage. Proceeding along Powder Mill Lane towards the Viaduct, there was a yard which contained a blacksmith's forge operated by a Mr Harmer and a coal business run by F.W. Butcher and Son. Mr Butcher was a local councillor serving the district on the SUDC. He also ran a garage at the yard. Over the building was a large loft, accessible by a flight of wooden stairs, which was occupied by the Salvation Army who held meetings there.

On the corner of Nursery Road and Powder Mill Lane was a small general and sweet shop run by Mr Startup; he had three sons, all good footballers, who played for the local team. Nursery Road had houses on both sides and on the left-hand side was a detached house occupied by two sisters called Mitchell. They ran a dairy from there and supplied the area with milk which came from their father's farm in the Vauxhall area. He was assisted by two sons, Harry and Eric. They also rented the field in Salisbury Road (now built on) and what is now the Frank Weare Recreational Ground.

Proceeding down Nursery Road, on the left side there was a small yard occupied by the Roland family, who lived in a caravan and sold second-hand furniture. A little further on, at the corner of Nursery Road and Colebrook Road, there was a clothiers and outfitters shop owned and run by a Mr Penney and his daughter, later by a Mr Leonard. On the opposite corner was an off-licence, selling beer in bottles or in a jug, also groceries. It was run by a Mr Chandler and his daughter and was later converted to a public house (in about 1936) and named the Long Bow by Kelsey the brewers.

Next door to the clothiers on Colebrook Road was a butcher's shop, run by Mr Langridge and family, one of five butchers in High Brooms. Next was a terrace of small shops, the first a fish and chip shop run by the Hartridge family: father, mother and two sons, Jim and Ted. They also had the next-door shop, which was a greengrocer's. The father was quite a character, well known in the district as Dick Hartridge. He owned a donkey and cart and a dog called Pincher who used to ride on the donkey's back. Dick used to go

Off-licence and corner shop on Nursery Road and Colebrook Road – it is now the Long Bow.

High Brooms School for Boys.

firewood. Then there were two shops, the first a general store run by Mr and Mrs Whitlock and the second, another butcher's shop, run by a Mr Quinnell.

Further along was a yard and stables used as a coal yard by George Luck and his son Alfred. About 1920 they sold the business to Robert Crouch and took on a farm in Powder Mill Lane, known as Forge Farm, which is now used as an abattoir, where they farmed for a number of years until giving over to a family called Smitherman. Going back to the yard, there were some outbuildings used as a foundry by a Mr Bullen, producing light metal work.

Proceeding down Colebrook Road, on the left side there was a greengrocer's shop run by the Cavie family. At the junction of Great Brooms Road was a yard used by gypsies during the winter months, living in caravans. Two names come to mind, Collins and Rossiter. When they were in residence, they used to deal in horses and would gallop them up and down for prospective buyers. Facing the yard was a field used by a Mr Simple who was, I believe, a butcher in Tunbridge Wells. At the bottom, near the edge of the clay pit, was a slaughter house, which used to kill cattle and sheep and pigs for the local and Tunbridge Wells butchers.

Opposite the gypsy yard was a footpath leading down to an old sandpit, which was known as the 'sand hole'; it was one of our play areas. The footpath was a private path leading to the brickyard (the lower end is now known as Baldwin's Lane) and it was closed for one day every year (always on Good Friday). It was manned at each end by a watchman to keep it private.

Going back to Powder Mill Lane, leaving High Brooms Road towards the Viaduct, on the left there was a sand-pit, run by Tom Hicks who also did some haulage work, where

every day except Sunday to Tunbridge Wells to buy fish at H. Jones, the wholesale fish merchant in Grosvenor Road, and sell it on the way home and around the local district. Next in the terrace was a chemist which sold patent medicines and toiletries. It was owned by Mr Watson, who had a chemist and optician's shop in Quarry Road, Tunbridge Wells, and anything not in stock in High Brooms could be obtained in a few hours from the Tunbridge Wells shop.

At the end of the row was a shoe repairer's run by a Mr Jenner. On the corner was an allotment, on which, later on, Pickfords built their furniture store-house. On the opposite side of Colebrook Road, there were houses and in one lived a Mr Jones who made 'pimps', small bundles of cleft wood used for lighting fires, and he also sold logs and the present school dining room now is. After that came the two schools mentioned earlier, then there was another sand-pit, run by a Mr Dinner and his son Jack. About 1,200 yards further down the lane were two cottages, one tenanted by a Miss or Mrs Millstead who ran a small poultry farm. Next was Forge Farm, run by the Luck family. Nearer the Viaduct was Broakes Farm, run by the Smith family, father and three sons. It was a dairy farm and they retailed their milk in the High Brooms and Tunbridge Wells area. At the rear of the farm was Broakes Mill, a watermill operated by a Mr Manuel. There was a mill pond which was filled by a stream from the North Farm area. There was a sluice gate which raised the level of water needed to work the water-wheel. In my time I only saw it operating once.

Off Powder Mill Lane was Salisbury Road; there were only about six houses and a building used by the International Order of Good Templars; the remainder was allotments. Back on Powder Mill Lane, opposite Hick's sand-pit, was Great Brooms Road. At the top was West Kent, or High Broom Villa, which had a large monkey puzzle tree in the garden. The villa was occupied by Mr and Mrs Young, who took in men boarders who worked at the gas or brick works on periodic maintenance work. Further down Great Brooms Road on the left was a yard owned by a Mr Piddlesden, who kept a few cows and used the barn in the yard to house them. George Goldsmith also kept cows and grazed them in the fields in the Yew Tree Road area. Next to the yard was a shop run by Mrs Piddlesden, who sold milk and eggs. Opposite that was Weare Road and on the corner was a general grocery store run by Mrs Barton. Weare Road at that time only had houses on the left-hand side; on the other side were allotments, where some people kept pigs

and poultry.

Going back to Great Brooms Road, there was a shop which was used as a small laundry run by a Mrs Young; afterwards it became a sweet and small grocery shop. To the left was Andrew Road; it had houses only on the left side and on the other side was Simple's field.

Back again to Great Brooms Road and there was the girls' school and opposite that was a small front-room shop run by a Mrs Martin, where you could buy sweets for as little as a farthing or you could buy small quantities of groceries, such as twopenn'orth of tea, 4oz of sugar and half a loaf of bread.

At the cross roads where Yew Tree Road runs into High Brooms Road was a baker's shop run by Mrs Harrison and bread was baked on the premises. It was also the post

The Long Bow pub today.

The logo of the High Brooms Brick Company, which provided the material for much of the housing in High Brooms.

office which was manned by the two sisters, the Misses Harrison. Further down High Brooms Road, on the right, was the Wesleyan chapel and after that a builder's yard owned by Mr P.F. Pankhurst. Next was a small building which housed a fire-fighting appliance, a hand-cart affair. Opposite that was a men's barber shop, run by Norman Strutt. Below that was a terrace of small shops opposite the parish hall. The first was a greengrocer, run by Mr and Mrs Webb, after that a newsagent's and barber shop run by a Mr McLeod, then a fish and chip shop which was later run by Bert Mallion who, in his spare time, was the local entertainer at clubs and children's parties. Then came another butcher's shop run by

Bert Owen and family, and lastly on the terrace there was a cycle repair shop which sold a variety of items. It was run by Jim Field, well known in the area and, if you wanted a helping hand, Jim was the one to supply it.

On the corner of High Brooms Road and Colebrook Road was the local baker's shop and bakehouse, run by Mr and Mrs F. Puckett and two sons, Arthur and Fred. They produced good bread and delivered it themselves round the district. Below them was another grocery and general store, run by Mr A. Goodyear and his son Ernest. On the corner across the road from the bakery was a large shop, with a house attached. I believe that it had been a grocery store but it was empty and unoccupied for a long time until it was taken on by a Miss Strange and used as a knitwear factory, employing about a dozen local women.

Next to it was Mr Newington's small newsagents but when he retired, it was turned into another butcher's shop, run by George Stoate. Then came St Matthew's church. Round the corner was Gordon Road, which had houses only on the right-hand side. The other side was waste ground, one of our many playgrounds. Further down was Wolseley Road and opposite that was Charlton's Nurseries, occupying quite a lot of ground. It was closed down in about 1935 and now forms the Welbeck Estate. The houses built on it were sold for around £500 and could be bought on a mortgage with a £50 deposit.

Next down the road was the High Brooms Hotel, owned, I think, by the Sussex brewers, Beards. Opposite was Stewart Road which had houses on one side only, with waste ground on the other side. On the bend, on the right-hand side, was the Working Men's Club, which was very popular and had a large membership. Below the hotel were two more shops; another butcher's shop run by a Mr

High Brooms Hotel, High Brooms Road.

Reg Norton with his dog outside Farrant's.

Carter and a newsagent and sweet shop run by Mr Rastron.

Opposite the station was G. Farrant's shop and yard. He was a coal merchant and corn chandler, and ran a substantial haulage business with horses and traction engines, doing a lot of work for the brickworks as well as timber haulage for the Baltic Saw Mills in Tunbridge Wells. Reg Norton married Mr Farrant's daughter and the Norton family still run the business today.

On the corner of High Brooms Road and North Farm Road was the Royal Kent Laundry which employed a large number of local females. Further along the road came the brick company's office and then three or four petrol company works. Petrol came in tankers to the railway sidings opposite and was pumped under the road to the storage tanks. It was then put into two gallon cans for delivery to garages and businesses over a large area. That was before the installation of petrol pumps.

Next came the brick yard. It was owned by the Weare family, Frank Weare, son Gerald and, after the war, the grandson of Frank. They made good quality bricks: Wire Cuts, Red Rustics, Golden Rustics, hand-made Silver Greys, Red and Bronze Staffordshires. They had their own railway siding and despatched bricks all over the country by rail and by horse and cart or steam traction engine locally. The works manager was a Mr Eddie Hicks and he was a very strict disciplinarian.

During the First World War, the yard was closed and taken over by the Army for use as a store. North Farm Road was closed and a relief road was made at the end of Clifton Road (east of the railway line) for the North Farm area.

At the end of North Farm Road was an iron foundry owned by a Mr Easterfield and later by Seale, Austen & Barnes of Tonbridge. Two of its principal workers were Jim and Bert Billson.

CHAPTER 3

Schooldays

The Revd Dr Reginald Bull, headmaster of St Andrew's School, and his wife, Agnes, in 1927.

St Andrew's Fire

Mr H.C. Luttman remembers St Andrew's School and the fire that almost cost him his life. He had only been at the school three weeks.

I had been at a school in Malvern Wells, not far from my home in Banbury, but I was not very happy there, and was a 'close-call'

victim of a measles epidemic. So in January 1919 I was moved to St Andrew's School – where I had an even closer call!

I remember little of the school during my short spell in Southborough, but I can never forget its dormitory in which I almost overslept. After the event, one can see what a hazard it was, partitioned into cubicles, having clapboard walls about seven feet high and doors opening onto a central passageway, so isolating each boy in a private – and readily inflammable – room.

The fire of February 8th was later attributed to an incubator in the basement, in which Mrs Bull hatched chickens. The alarm was sounded and the boys filed out into a bitter night and down the driveway to the lodge on the main road. A roll call revealed that I, the only new boy that term, was missing. Kenneth Ball, known as Captain Kenneth and the son of the school's headmaster, the Revd Dr Reginald A. Bull, heroically went to find me.

I was first conscious of being out of bed, with Kenneth trying to get me into my dressing gown. The lights were on, in a fog of smoke, above the cubicle walls. Since I was too 'new' to have done any fire drill, Kenneth thought it best not to risk my panicking on the fire escape ladder, by which I believe he had climbed into the dormitory. Taking my hand, he whisked me down the stairs.

Flames were already licking around them and there was a lot of smoke but, thank God, the lights were still on. I remember gasping 'Oh Sir! Oh Sir!' as we rushed down. Some bagatelle boards had fallen across the foot of the stairs and we tripped over them. Picking ourselves up, we reached the front door and out into the night, later described in a schoolboy essay as 'so cold that the water froze in the firemen's nozzles'.

My hair was singed a little but otherwise I was unscathed. Kenneth had cut his hand breaking the glass to get into the dormitory from the fire escape. We were very lucky.

People across the road generously put us all up in their sitting rooms for the night, and our families – my aunts from Seal Chart – collected us next day. So ended my education in Southborough.

The phoenix rose from the ashes quickly and the school reopened in Hammerwood House near East Grinstead within a few weeks and then after a few terms moved to Yewhurst, near Forest Row, which was a big house once owned by Sir Abe Bailey.

Dr Bull, the headmaster, was scholarly and kindly, and several boys had Church connections; at least one of my contemporaries became a bishop. Dr Bull's wife, Agnes, though all honey to our parents was – *nihil nisi bonum* – rather a dragon to us boys.

St Andrew's was a very happy school, with a moderate emphasis on religion. We were reminded of the several instances – for example John VI, verse 9 and XII, verse 22 – of people being brought to Christ by St Andrew. Each morning we learned a few verses of the Gospels, to echo for the rest of our lives, and most of us were confirmed in the School chapel.

The chapel escaped the fire in Southborough and we were given the impression it was taken down and moved to Yewhurst. I think it more likely, however, that only the windows, moveable fittings and perhaps the pews were transferred.

In such a healthy moral atmosphere, discipline could be light and, while boys will be boys, I remember no serious misbehaviour or flouting of the spirit of the school motto – *Tenax Propositi* – Firm of Purpose.

Classes were small and the teaching was generally sympathetic; perhaps there was a tendency towards the Classics rather than the modern side. My own interests lay in English more than anything else. Apart from school work, we had other cultural activities, such as formal debates, dramatics and choral performances. We were very fortunate, at Yewhurst, in having a superb

Firemen inspect the burnt-out remains of St Andrew's School and the frozen water from their hoses.

cricket field – used by visiting South African XIs in Sir Abe Bailey's day – and sports of all sorts were encouraged.

The school had an admirable merit system, called Stars and Stripes. A large board listed all the boys and, opposite each, a double row of squares. Meritorious performance, from a poem to a hat-trick, was awarded a quarter Star, a half Star, or even a full Star, and a square on the board was appropriately marked in red pencil. A demerit, from consistent inattention in class to a deliberate foul on the football field, earned a Stripe, and a square was filled in blue pencil. The red and blue rows ran neck and neck (it took a full Star to balance a Stripe) and when the red was, I think, three Stars ahead at the end of a term, one got a leather-bound book prize. For some benign reason Stripes never seemed to get too far ahead!

There was no school uniform as such, except for a school cap with a St Andrew's cross, in light blue, across the top of it. Mrs Bull was a diligent knitter and made football jerseys, dark blue with a light blue collar, for all the boys. They were rather a loose weave but rugged enough for schoolboy soccer.

The food was adequate, insofar as the schoolboys ever considered food adequate, though we often cast envious eyes at the spread on 'head table'. It would have been kinder to feed the staff separately and remotely from the boys. I remember that for one meal we were rationed to two bits of bread and butter and two bits of bread and jam, spread very thinly, augmented by slices of dry bread, passed around on a plate by a waitress.

I went on to Marlborough College in January 1922; an unexpected vacancy occurred after I had left St Andrew's for the Christmas holidays. I think it says something for Dr Bull's interest in his boys that, when he learned I would not be coming back, he arranged with my parents that I should visit him for one night, so he could say good-bye and complete my primary education with a quiet talk about the birds and the bees or, in blunter terms, 'the facts of life'!

I last saw Dr Bull in 1937, when I was stationed in Manchester by the Air Ministry and drove over to see him, in retirement, somewhere in North Wales. Kenneth, his son, had taken over as headmaster. I speak no Welsh but I could translate the name of his little house which, to Anglo-Saxon ears, sounded like 'Llys Andreas'.

High Brooms Girls' School

High Brooms Girls' School was founded in 1890 and had four houses: Alexandra, Cavell, Nightingale and Darling. A much-loved headmistress was Miss M.L. (Linda) Webb who had been a pupil at Tunbridge Wells Girls' Grammar before studying at the Royal Holloway College and Whitelands Training College. In 1936, Miss Webb took over the school from Miss K. Austin who had been head since 1900. Miss Webb retired in 1960. During one Prize Giving in the late 1950s, Miss Webb reported to the girls, parents and governors about the past school year's activities. Her address helps to explain her own, and the school's, ethos. (I am indebted to Angela Rowbottom of Yew Tree Road for this account).

During the last two years at school a vocational interest enters into the curriculum. An effort is made to interpret the outside world of adult-wage earning work by visits and discussions, and all the courtesies such as introductions and thanks, spoken or written, in connection with these arrangements provide excellent material for work in school. Thoroughness and scholarliness are ideals which we need to defend today; the pendulum has swung so far in the direction of making learning pleasant, that we are in danger of taking the backbone out of it. I want the girls to enjoy learning, but I hold no brief for not persevering with the dull routine of work that must be done, even though difficult, nor with leaving any job unfinished, once it is begun.

Mrs Collin has played her part in teaching the commercial group book-keeping and commercial English and, under Mrs Hoyte, the girls have made good progress with their French. The new

Miss M.L. Webb, headmistress of High Brooms Girls' School from 1936 to 1960.

Miss Webb welcomes back the evacuees following the doodlebug scare of December 1944.

Miss Webb, former head of High Brooms Girls' School, with some girls in Victorian costume on 17 May 1980. The occasion was an exhibition to celebrate the ninetieth anniversary of the school. The girls are, from left to right, back row: Sandra Luxford, Karen Moore, Juliet Docherty, Lisa Mills. Front row: Amanda Vanns, Andrea Luker, Diane Delay.

needlework scheme has been carried out by Miss Gingell ... and she has been able to inculcate the right attitude of common sense, thought and thoroughness. The seeing eye must be also the choosing and discriminating eye, and we have this cultivation of taste in mind, hoping it will lead to good home-making and house-keeping in the future.

Miss Parker continues to inculcate these same powers of thoroughness and discrimination in her weaving and book-binding courses. The girls have experienced the joy and satisfaction gained from a piece of craft well done.

The Young Farmers' Club has received a new lease of life under the leadership of Mrs Miles and a talk has been given on the fascinating history of horse brasses and several visits have been made. Unfortunately the two farm visits had to be cancelled because of foot and mouth disease.

Miss Gingell and Mrs Miles working together have produced a fine crop of swimmers which accounts for the 73 certificates of various kinds, including life saving, to be presented today.

In Mrs Heselton's classes, dramatic movement, mimes and short scenes for groups ... are proving a useful means of stimulating interest, especially with self-conscious girls. This subject involves teamwork, self-control and a lively imagination, as well as the ability to put oneself in the other fellow's shoes, so it increases understanding and tolerance. Imagination is a God-given gift but it needs cultivating.

I should like to pay a tribute, too, to Miss Powell and her staff who continue to put such good and appetising dinners before us. I thought all the girls looked very fit at the Baths last week, and decided that Miss Powell has nearly given some of us a need for slimming.

Holden Park School

Holden Park School was founded in 1891 by the former headmaster of St Peter's School for Boys, Mr Edward Fletcher. He opened a Higher Grade Boarding and Day School for boys at what is now 60 Holden Park Road. In 1898 the school moved around the corner to Holden Park House which is now 61 Prospect Road. It moved premises at least once more after that and took both boys and girls. Alan C. Waters, who now lives in Tonbridge, was born and brought up in Southborough. His family had the greengrocery business in Bedford Road. Alan attended the school during the Second World War.

I started at Holden Park School soon after my fourth birthday in the autumn of 1943. It did not strike me as strange that this school was very small, having only about a dozen pupils, both boys and girls, and was held in the front bedroom of Miss Johnston's house at 22 Vale Road. The hours were from 9 a.m. until 1 p.m.; thus we had every afternoon free, much to the envy of some of my friends who attended the school on the Common –

which we referred to as the common school with a small 'c'. We wore maroon blazers with the emblem HPS on the pocket, which my mother explained stood for Holden Park School, though why it should be so called when it was a long way from Holden Park Road always puzzled me; I now know. Other local children thought differently and would call after us 'Heinz Pork Sausages'.

My memory of the school is patchy but I do recall Miss Johnston. She was a very upright lady, with a mass of silver hair, who maintained order by working us hard, but I never remember her having to shout or smack in order to do so. She held the belief that what children needed in their first few years of school was to learn the three Rs. Thus we spent no time learning any of the arts but concentrated on simple arithmetic, reading and writing. On the rear wall of the classroom were the tables – two times up to twelve; sometimes we chanted these but often Miss Johnston would make us turn our backs on them and she would go round the class asking question: 'Alan Waters, six times nine?'

Miss Johnston totally disagreed with the then new idea of teaching children to print and introduce them to script later. When Hitler's terror weapons began to fall on our part of Kent, my mother became rather worried at the closeness of some of the doodlebugs and decided to evacuate to Cornwall, where I attended a village school near Penryn. This was my first encounter with educational lunacy, as I was told that children of my age don't do 'joined-up writing', they print, and so I had to learn to print. When I returned to Miss Johnston's, she called my mother to the school and expressed her displeasure at the state of my writing, and so I had to re-learn to write in script! Even today I find the odd printed letter creeping into my handwriting.

School during the war was interrupted frequently by the air-raid warning siren. When this happened we all stood, picked up the cardboard boxes containing our gas masks and filed quietly downstairs to a large lobby under the stairs, where we stayed until the 'all clear'. These spells under the stairs were not wasted. Miss Johnston would stand in the doorway and conduct an impromptu class in mental arithmetic.

We were encouraged to read at home and Miss Johnston would tell parents quite firmly that she expected her pupils to own their own books and that parents should help their children by reading to them each evening before going to bed. Now, as most of the fathers were away serving in the Armed Forces, this burden fell on the mothers, but they did it. I think that they held Miss Johnston in awe as much as we did.

The more senior pupils were sometimes allowed to study unsupervised downstairs in Miss Johnston's front room, usually to work on more difficult sums or perhaps write a story. The strange thing was that nobody took advantage of the situation; we just quietly got on with our work.

We had no break, or 'playtime' as most children called it, as there was no playground. Instead we would stop work and two pupils would be delegated to go

Holden Park House, Southborough, at the turn of the twentieth century.

Holden Park School in 1918. Mr and Mrs Fletcher were the principals. (Courier photograph)

downstairs and carry up the milk bottles, and others to get the mugs out. Miss Johnston would then measure out our allowance and we had to drink it in front of her and then get back to our work. This was the only part of school I disliked, as I detested milk (and still do) but, under Miss Johnston's firm gaze, there was no argument. Early on I can remember that I did voice a protest but she just smiled and said 'drink it, please', which didn't leave much room for further debate.

It wasn't until I had left Holden Park School that I realised what a superb education I had received in those early years. When I was about seven or eight, I went to High Brooms School for Boys and remember being shocked to find that none of the children could write in script – back to printing for me! – and only about half the class could read even simple books. By this time Enid Blyton (yet to fall from favour) and several other authors were producing a

good range of children's books, but few in the class could manage them. The same was true of arithmetic; I could cope with long division and simple fractions but in this I was alone. I cannot help but wonder that, if Miss Johnston's system was employed today, our children might benefit. My memory of Holden Park School is that, whilst we worked hard, it was a thoroughly enjoyable experience. All her pupils left, at about age seven, masters of the three Rs.

The Ridgewaye School

Mr C.J. Rogers was the third headmaster of Ridgewaye School, from 1969 to 1988. The first headmaster, Mr G.H. Robinson, was appointed in November 1955 and the first pupils, boys and girls, arrived the following year. It closed in 1991. Mr Rogers recalls the school's success and the political machinations that led to its closure.

Ridgewaye School was one of the new schools built to cope with the increase in the post-war birth rate. In January 1956, 405 boys and girls were admitted. The original buildings soon proved to be inadequate and by 1959 three more classrooms had been built. By 1960 a further six classrooms were added and a new gymnasium came into use in 1961. By this time the number of pupils had risen to over 550.

There was a temporary decline in numbers in the mid-sixties because fewer children had been born in the mid-fifties. This did not discourage Ridgewaye and efforts to improve facilities continued. School fêtes were held and an appeal to improve the school stage had been launched. Planning for a new outdoor swimming pool was in progress. Workshop facilities were extended and a new Rural Science unit was in use.

Gradually numbers began to increase again and pupils were coming to Ridgewaye from Tonbridge and Hildenborough. The Hildenborough parents even chartered their own coach to make the journey easier for their children.

In those days children were allowed to leave school at fifteen years, but Ridgewaye built up a sizeable fifth form aiming at the new Certificate of Secondary Education (CSE) and a modest sixth form aiming at GCE O-level.

Mr Banks, as head of Mathematics, was already attracting attention to his development of what was soon to be called Ridgewaye Mathematics, later West Kent Mathematics. Eventually it became the Kent Mathematics Project and Mr Banks became full-time Project Director, with Ridgewaye as the lead school demonstrating the work. Visitors were soon coming from all over this country and before long they were arriving from Australia, New Zealand, Canada, the USA and India as well as from European countries. As Kent Mathematics Project spread to other Kent schools, Ridgewaye had to ask other schools to share in receiving some of the visitors. A short time before his death (1993), Mr Banks published a book recording the development of his work and the involvement of Ridgewaye School.

Mr G.H. Robinson, who had been the first headmaster, had guided the school with the help of his deputy, Mr A.W. Pease, through over thirteen years of eventful development, when he left at Easter 1969 to open Rede School in Rochester. Mr Pease, who had been deputy since Ridgewaye opened, was then acting head until I arrived in September 1969.

In 1973 the school leaving age was raised to sixteen and Ridgewaye's full sized fifth form helped raise numbers to just under 600. A new block had been built near the swimming pool and the demand for places was increasing, but Ridgewaye was not permitted to take more than a four-form entry of about 120 pupils each year. Local children were given priority, but it was hard to turn away applicants from Hildenborough and Tonbridge and the more distant parts of Tunbridge Wells, especially when there were family links with older brothers and sisters who had already been at Ridgewaye. It was also difficult when families had just moved into Southborough or High Brooms only to find that there was no space in their local school for their children.

A further population increase forced Kent to change its policy in 1976 and Ridgewaye was at last permitted to take a five-form entry. Within three years there were 700 children in the school. One by one six 'mobiles' were provided to accommodate

The Ridgewaye School's production of Oliver! *in 1974. The principal members of the cast were: L. Rogers (Oliver), G. Mewis (Fagin), A. Comben (Artful Dodger), B. Hazelton (Bill Sykes), J. Clark (Nancy), H. Coultrup (Bet), C. Oulton (Mr Bumble), J. Cuthbert (Mrs Corney), A. Warren (Mr Brownlow), D. Neve (Mr Sowerberry), L. Piper (Mrs Sowerberry), P. Burns (Charlotte), J. Peyton (Noah Claypole), P. Harman (Dr Grimwig), K. Collison (Mrs Bedwin), T. Clifton (Old Sally), B. Rich (Charley Bates).*

the extra classrooms on the school grounds.

Ridgewaye was fortunate in attracting not only many highly talented pupils and wonderfully supportive parents, but also a great number of remarkably gifted and hard-working teachers. So much happened, in and after school hours: educational visits to other parts of Britain and Europe, Duke of Edinburgh Awards (the first Golds were achieved in 1970), work experience for all the fifteen-year-olds for one whole week in the post-examination period after the summer exams, pioneer work in Kent to develop Certificate of Pre-Vocational Education and special exhibitions like European Week in 1982 and Roman Week in 1984.

Academic and examination work flourished to the extent that A-levels were introduced in 1981 and in 1983 the school was rewarded by being able to send its first pupil from the Sixth form to a Polytechnic. In 1984 another pupil got two grade Bs and a grade C and gained a place at Birmingham University. These, and all the others who followed them, were pupils who had been unable to gain grammar school places at the eleven-plus.

Dramatic productions were played to packed audiences. Many will remember *Animal Farm, Lord of the Flies, Oliver!* and *Charlie and the Chocolate Factory*, just three of the many productions with music and

*The main block of Ridgewaye School, 1988. (*Courier *photograph)*

songs written by the school staff. The Kart Club attracted large numbers of boys and girls and parents eager to share in making and driving the karts in out-of-school time.

Sports were not neglected. Several talented girls played hockey for Kent under-16 and under-18 teams and one played for England Women's under-18 team. Boys who were keen on indoor-football swept the board for several years, winning the area league championship and sportsmanship awards. A full range of activities was available – not only the traditional games, but also fencing, croquet, rock-climbing, sailing and horse-riding.

Ridgewaye also undertook a great deal of community service work, almost all in out-of-school hours, and for several years grants were awarded by the National Westminster Bank project 'Respond' to assist the community groups receiving the school's help. The most spectacular publicity was achieved in 1979 when Ridgewaye School's entry won the BBC Nationwide Carol Competition.

Such efforts and achievements had the effect of attracting applicants for school places from a wide radius which reduced the applicants for places in rival schools. In 1980 the authorities made the school reduce its intake to four-form entry again. There were many protests and because the Government was promoting the principle of market forces, in 1982 Kent said 'Open Enrolment' should prevail. Once again Ridgewaye was allowed to take all applicants and numbers rose to just under 700 the same year.

To complicate matters further, the birth-rate had been declining and the number of children coming through the primary schools was falling. Ridgewaye hoped to maintain its popularity, but by 1984 there were too many empty spaces in rival schools and Kent made yet another U-turn and limited the school to four-form entry yet again. Primary school pupils were being encouraged to apply to other secondary schools where class sizes were smaller. Restrictions on travelling allowances were applied by Kent. Pupils from Fordcombe and Bidborough were told that travelling allowance would only be paid to pupils going to Tonbridge schools, while those living in Langton Green, Ramslye, Showfields and Rusthall would only receive travelling assistance if they went to Sandown Court.

When Ridgewaye numbers began to decline, it seemed reasonable to ask to return to 'a level playing field' and a system that did not discriminate against any school. Kent Education Committee would not agree to change its policy, and even though the birth rate was continuing to decline, it was still a shock for parents and staff alike to read in the local press in January 1988 that Huntleys School in Tunbridge Wells and Ridgewaye were to close. When the Education Committee confirmed this, it became clear that this had been part of a design. It explained why there had been strangers walking about the school site without reporting to the school office. Clearly there were estimates being made of the market value of the Ridgewaye site. It was explained that Southborough and High Brooms children would be expected to fill empty spaces in Sandown Court or the Tonbridge schools of Hayesbrook and Hillview. Economies must be made and some schools had to close.

Staff and parents and pupils mounted a tremendous campaign with the support of the governors led by Mrs Elizabeth Garlick and with some help from Sir Patrick Mayhew. I was due to retire in the summer of 1988, but it was heart-warming to see the efforts being made to try to ensure the survival of Southborough's secondary school.

The campaign led to a directive from the Government that Kent should reconsider its plans for West Kent. In September Mr F.J. Jurriaanse, who had been deputy head since Mr Pearse's retirement in 1980, became headmaster with Mrs N. Merriman as senior deputy head and Miss D.J.B. Balesworth and Mr H.P. Swan became deputy heads also. They faced the difficult task of running the school and maintaining morale with the drive, energy and enthusiasm which had characterized life at Ridgewaye for so many years.

Hopes were eventually dashed again when, in due course, it became clear that Kent's policy would lead inexorably to closure and that Ridgewaye would not be allowed to accept any more intake from primary schools.

It was a sad conclusion, that with the changing patterns in birth-rate, Ridgewaye School had become a victim of its own success and of the U-turns in the county's education policy and of the potential value of the school grounds if they were put on the market. In spite of this, many thousands of past pupils, parents and friends of the school will remember the successes and achievements of thirty-five memorable years.

'Aim High for Excellence'

Mrs Susan Phillips (née Turley) lives in Broomhill Park Road; she remembers her time at Ridgewaye School, which she attended between 1966 and 1970.

Having come from the cosy community of the tiny school on the Common behind St Peter's church, I entered the gates of Ridgewaye School in September 1966 in some trepidation. My brother John was in the fourth year and three out of five of my other siblings – Margaret, Linda and Raymond – had also been there before me. My 'new girl' status no doubt displayed itself in my unblemished appearance – grey pleated skirt, white blouse, bright red cardigan, red and gold tie and grey blazer emblazoned with the school emblem of bow, arrow and book. The motto as I remember it was: 'Aim High for Excellence.'

The vast grounds, endless corridors and stairways were all rather daunting, as was the first assembly with the headmaster, Mr G.H. Robinson, who presided over us in a black gown worn over his suit, which in much later days always aroused comments like: 'Here comes Batman.' He was always affectionately known as 'Scrom', but to this day I have no idea why.

A few other teachers of that era had their own nicknames. There was Binkie Warren, Noddy Knight, Colonel Rose and Jock Petty, the last being the boys' PE teacher. That was one time in my life when I was glad to be female, as his reputation as a taskmaster had gone before him. However, as the weeks progressed, everything fell into a routine.

One of the lessons I enjoyed was Rural Studies. Oliver Brooks, the teacher, used to march us in regimental fashion from the main building to the hut near Crendon Park entrance, where there was a wildlife pond, gardens and chicken coop. I used to enjoy collecting the eggs and just generally being outside for a change.

I was very fortunate to be taught maths by Mr Banks and was one of the first to participate in his Kent Maths Project (KMP) scheme, which came to be widely used in schools here and abroad. Cookery was something of a hit and miss with me; anything that turned out OK was usually eaten by my brother-in-law, who could stomach some of the more unusual dishes my family were not used to. I remember one disaster was a loaf which my brother John hurled up the path, where it landed with a thud. Even the birds snubbed it.

Break times in summer were spent sitting under the large trees in the grounds by the sports field enjoying the dappled sunshine, exchanging the latest news with my peers or watching a rare fight, which we called a 'bundle', going on in the playground.

The hockey pitch was opposite the school in Hill Crest. Many were the icy cold days I spent there in preference to puffing around Southborough on cross country. However I was quite proud to represent my house, Weavers, on Sports Day in javelin, discus and shot. The other houses were Brokes, Broom and Fishers. Rivalry was fierce but friendly. House points for good work were also awarded. Prize Giving was an annual event and I was proud to receive a book myself in my last year which I still have, along with autographs of teachers and pupils.

Once a year the school fête was held in the grounds and was always well attended, and I don't know if it's just me but the weather as I remember was always hot! I was fortunate to be at the school when the outdoor swimming pool was built. It was quite small and enclosed by a fence but we thought it was wonderful.

In my last year I recall we were allowed discos in the canteen area outside the staff rooms after school on Fridays, which were much enjoyed. A gathering place after school was the corner of Yew Tree Road and The Ridgewaye. The owner of that house must have found our presence and litter a constant nuisance.

We were blessed with some very good teachers, and I hope the nicknames won't offend any of those still with us. I know that this will bring back memories for many pupils from that time and later. Colonel Rose would often play tapes in English which were sometimes rather boring and we would will the clock round to 3.50 p.m., 'going home time'. Noddy Knight was so enthusiastic about his poetry that, if anyone dare interrupt, they would be sent out of the room, and he would continue until the next interruption. 'Out!' he would shout, and on again. He was seemingly oblivious to his surroundings and, by the end of the lesson, often more pupils were outside the class than were in it. Binkie Warren was a jolly

Pupils at the Ridgewaye School, 1969. From left to right, back row: Stephen Pring, Stephen Medhurst, Michael Dews, David Austen, Barry Clements, Colin Jackson. Middle row: Michael Sawyer, John Salter, Kevin Collard, Wendy Lower, Diane Neve, Gillian Lower, Teresa Westguard, Paul Kourellious, Kevin Sole, Brian Kent. Front row: Joanne Keegan, Amanda Kemp, Susan Roser, Prunella Everard, Sally Barrett, Alison Cowie, Gillian Beeny, Jacqueline Davis, Valerie Hawkes.

man with a mop of dark curly hair and dark-rimmed glasses. He was a good geography teacher; well, he gave me A grades, so I might be biased. Miss Collins didn't have a nickname. When she entered the room her very presence would create a deathly hush, as she was not one to tolerate misbehaviour.

The saddest days of my time at Ridgewaye were losing my best friend Linda Seal, who died aged thirteen, and another pupil in my year, Colin Puttock. I left the Ridgewaye in 1970 and went to work in Post Office Telegrams. In September 1991, I attended the school reunion and met some of my old friends, though not as many as I would have liked. I did find a poem in print there that my brother Raymond had written and, since he had died in 1960, when I was only five, I found this particularly poignant.

After its closure Ridgewaye School soon became a victim of vandalism, and the broken windows and overgrown hedges were a sorry sight indeed. Now, when I walk past and see that the old school has been replaced by houses, I smile to myself and think : 'You can knock down a school but my treasured memories can never be erased.'

Ormonde Lodge

George Paine was born in 1904 and before he died in 1998 he wrote down a number of reminiscences for the Southborough Society. Here he recalls Ormonde Lodge before and during the First World War. This was a fine house that formerly stood on the site of what is now the Meadows School on the Sceptre Hill.

The name Ormonde Lodge was rarely used by the locals; we more often referred to it as 'Missopes', the then owner being an elegant lady called Miss Hope, daughter of a retired Naval officer. The building always seemed to me as if it had been transported from the front at Brighton, beautifully proportioned double-bay frontage with a hint of Regency in the steps and a porchway. Miss Hope had, I believe, a social connection with Miss Harland (of Harland and Wolff shipyard fame), the resident owner of Great Boundes. I recall something of a 'shindy' among some of the cricketers of the day when to claim having hit a six which reached the front door of Ormonde Lodge was considered the ultimate challenge for a batsman.

The main gate was guarded by a tiny lodge in which lived two old brothers, Brown by name. They were also responsible for the upkeep of St Peter's churchyard. My wife, Kathleen, born in the School House behind the church, remembered them as two kindly old white-bearded men who would hand to her as a little girl over the fence any wax ornamental flowers from a broken grave decoration. She treasured them and placed them on her little rockery. She thought of these old men as Moses and Aaron!

The house was saved from demolition by the 1914-1918 war. On the departure of Miss Hope, the whole of the premises was taken over by the Army. They were at first a company of signallers mounted on bicycles. The Common became festooned with wire among the higher branches of the oak and pine trees. Many of the lads of the town became adept at making 'tapper and buzzer' sets with the old Le Clanché cells to work them (the torch battery had not yet arrived). We would watch and listen avidly as a Sergeant Instructor taught a bunch of recruits using the Morse code, or instructed them on mounting and operating a heliograph. From the middle of the cricket

Ormonde Lodge, which was demolished around 1935.

pitch the mirror would light up the church clock face – an imaginary distant station.

I can only recall passing through the gates of Ormonde Lodge twice. The first time was when we helped Mr Penticost collect his cows from the lady's front garden. They had made short work of the flowerbed in the roundel in the driveway. Those cows were by 'common-right' allowed to wander and roam the grass on the Common, often crossing the main road to enjoy the sweet young grass in the stretch in front of Ormonde Lodge and Stuart Cottage. Imagine such a thing happening today. The drinking trough was in constant use. Mr Penticost farmed at Modest Corner and kept a dairy herd.

The second visit occurred much later, during the First War period. I cannot be certain but I believe the signallers left for France and the house and paddock were occupied by a company, or more, of infantry – the Somerset Light Infantry comes to mind. Many troops were billeted in cottages and other dwellings around the whole town. Food rationing became easier if you housed a couple of soldiers! Ormonde Lodge was still, of course, the Headquarters, with the nearby Hand & Sceptre Hotel as, so to speak, the nineteenth hole for the officers.

As a twelve-year-old schoolboy walking home from Tonbridge in cadet uniform, I saw an Army motorcyclist drop, inadvertently, a package from his rear carrier. Feeling not a little heroic, I explained to the sentry at Ormonde Lodge gate, and was escorted to the guardroom just inside the front door. A grinning sergeant disillusioned my idea that I had rescued an important military document, by hinting that the parcel was probably the Adjutant's trousers returned from the tailor!

We boys would watch, goggle-eyed, the vicious attacks by fixed bayonets on a line of swinging straw-stuffed bodies just over the hedge of the paddock. The colourful language of the instructors, egging on the raw recruits, I regret to say added to our entertainment.

Several military exercises were carried out between the Regular troops and the then 'Dad's Army', known as the Kent Volunteer Force. My father-in-law to be, Mr W.F.A. Cox, the school headmaster at St Peter's, in one such challenge with a fellow comrade, dressed as a courting couple, penetrated the Ormonde Lodge defences but they were ruled out of order!

A final story involves a white donkey. This little fellow was at one time used to pull a rather grand bath-chair belonging to Miss Harland, for which purpose a mown grass track was made through the Great Boundes Park almost to Bidborough.

He was, in due course, pensioned off and Miss Hope agreed to give him sanctuary in her paddock to end his days in peace. Sadly, although he became the pet mascot, so to speak, of the Regiment, too many young soldiers on his back at one time caused a fatal injury. He had to be put down. I know this, as I saw him brought on a knacker's cart to our farm in the Ridgewaye. Somewhere, in somebody's private garden, lie the remains of the little white donkey.

Maxwell Macfarlane completes the Ormonde Lodge story.

Ormonde Lodge continued as a private residence until at least 1929, when the last known occupant was a Mr Benjamin Cox. By 1932, it had become an annexe of Fosse Bank Girls' School in Tonbridge and continued as such until 1935, when it became High Ormonde Girls' School, under a Miss M. Scott. However, this establishment did not last very long and there is no mention of Ormonde Lodge in the Kelly's Directory of 1936, 1937 or 1939, during which the original building must have been demolished because in 1940, there appears an entry for the Meadows Memorial Home, a branch of Dr Barnardo's Homes.

Dr Thomas John Barnardo was born in Dublin in 1845. A clerk by profession, he was converted to Christianity in 1862, and after a spell preaching in the Dublin slums went to London in 1866 to study medicine with the aim of becoming a medical missionary. Instead, he founded, while still a student, the East End Mission for destitute children in Stepney in 1867. After that followed a number of homes, starting in 1870 with one for destitute boys and in 1876 one for girls. He died in 1905 and currently there are over 100 Dr Barnardo's Homes in Britain and abroad.

Mike Price, who used to work at Meadows, takes up the story.

Captain Thomas Meadows, a merchant seaman who had himself been a 'Barnardo's boy', left money in his will which was used to build a home in his memory. The home originally had seventy to eighty Barnardo boys, who attended local schools, and it was managed by a superintendent.

After the Second World War, a property adjacent to Birchwood Garage called Windy Edge (formerly part of the Holme School) was purchased, with the campus acting as a staging post for pupils who were being offered a new start in Australia and Canada. In 1951, because of considerable social change, the home changed to become more like a school with a superintendent-headmaster in charge. Premises were

A horse-trough on Sceptre Hill presented by Sir David Salomons in 1894.

developed to enable elementary education to be undertaken on site rather than in the local schools and later Broomfields on Vicarage Road was purchased.

A single-storey lower school was constructed as well as a gymnasium and Meadows became a residential special school, catering for children with a wide range of behavioural problems and difficult social backgrounds – the occupancy went down to between forty and fifty pupils.

Some time after 1973, the superintendent-headmaster became known as the principal and George Wyllie fulfilled this role with distinction until he retired in 1994. Under his guidance, Meadows brought other properties within Southborough and Tunbridge Wells to enable the pupils to be resident off the main school site and participate in a non-institutional environment. During this purchasing phase

a decision was taken to admit day pupils and girls; co-education started in 1984.

As long ago as 1980 it was identified that the physical environment of Meadows School needed to be considerably developed to ensure continued success within the field of special education. Various plans were considered and rejected between 1983 and 1990. Restructuring of the building to allow effective education did not seem a viable proposition and it was decided to raze the building to the ground and start from scratch with a custom-built school. Barnardo's architect department developed plans for a modern efficient building based on a Kentish oast house design. A National Appeal was started to raise funds to offset the £2.4 million development cost.

During the transition from 'Old' Meadows to 'New' Meadows, alternative educational accommodation was urgently

Barnardo's boys returning to Meadows School after a run, c. 1965.

required – Knotley Hall at Chiddingstone Causeway was the only viable proposition. This building had been unoccupied for three years and required considerable refurbishment; however, it remained a dark and dismal place for the three years it took to build and equip the new school. Pupils and staff deserve considerable praise for maintaining a viable education resource in what was a totally unsuitable site.

On 31 January 1992, a foundation stone was laid at Southborough by Dr George Carey, Archbishop of Canterbury and Vice President of Barnardo's. Eventually, the great day dawned in September 1993 when pupils started the autumn term in the new Meadows School, a school developed with the twenty-first century in mind, which is able to cater for up to fifty-six children. The

educational and social difficulties that the pupils at Meadows present demand a high staff ratio – twelve teachers, twenty-six residential social workers and a host of ancillary staff service the needs of the pupils.

Meadows School has a long relationship with the people of Southborough and the newest pupil and staff member is soon aware of the bond that exists between the town and the school.

The first superintendent was Revd E.W. McKeeman, then Christopher G. Hensby took over in 1947 and was in charge until 1963. Reginald S. Davies was superintendent-headmaster from 1964 to 1973 when the aforementioned George Wyllie became principal. I was principal from 1994 to 1995 since when the school has been run by Robert Schoedel.

CHAPTER 4

Work

A watercolour by C.T. Dodd of Broakes Mill, painted in 1848. The original is in Tunbridge Wells Museum.

Broakes Mill

Broakes Mill in Powdermill Lane was remembered by Mr A.G. King of 12 Grecian Road, Tunbridge Wells in 1979. Broakes Mill had been an industrial site since the middle of the sixteenth century when iron was first smelted and forged there. The hammer for the iron foundry was worked by a waterwheel as were the bellows for the furnace. Following this the mill was used to make gunpowder – hence the name Powdermill Lane – and then corn milling succeeded gunpowder manufacturing by 1845. In 1907 Lewis Manuel became the miller and continued grinding corn for the local bakeries until the mill closed in 1923.

In 1904 my family moved from 10 Taylor Street to the cottages at the bottom of Powdermill Lane. The miller, Mr Manuel, had a small house on the west side of the mill. There were two mill ponds, one on the right hand side of the lane and one on the left; these were filled from a stream coming from High Brooms which ran much faster than it does now. The actual beds of the mill ponds are now filled with trees, but I used to spend many happy hours watching the swans go sailing majestically to and fro.

The right-hand pond was more than ten or twenty times larger than that on the left hand side because Mr Manuel needed a plentiful supply of water to turn those huge grinding stones to make the flour. Of course he could not grind at any time he liked although there was a good flow of water in those days; during the winter the stream would almost get out of control. I can remember him grumbling when he had to get up in the middle of the night to open the floodgate to stop the water flowing over the road and washing it away. Then the pond on the left hand side came into its real use as it eased the flow as it then rushed past the mill; it also had to be controlled when Mr Manuel wanted to do some grinding or it would make the waterwheel go too fast. Of course in the summer it would be almost the reverse, but I can say in truth that Mr Manuel knew how to treat that old pond.

Inside, the mill was very dark, you had to learn your way around. Just inside the door was the bin for the ground floor and to the left of this was a place where the sacks were filled and weighed. Further to the left and forward was the waterwheel control; this wheel is now very rusty but you can still see the remains of the troughs or buckets as they were called which caught the water as it fell from the height of about four to six feet. Then on the right inside the mill was a flight of stairs which led to the centre pin of the grindstones. During my school holidays

I spent many happy days helping Mr Manuel but I was still a small boy. I could only carry empty sacks around and generally clean up. In return for these services he would take me with the horse and cart delivering flour to the local bakers.

Mr Manuel was a keen amateur photographer and had an old fashioned camera with a tripod and a black cloth over the back. He used to ask me if I could see the 'dicky bird'. I feel sure there should be some photos of the mill around. Next door to the mill there was a family by the name of Smith who had the farm which stretched up past our cottages, and under the viaduct was a farmer by the name of Darck.

Redcar Buses

A lady still living in Southborough (her father was born in 1860 so it gives you an idea of how venerable she is!) used to work for James Bogue Elliott who founded, with his brothers Yule and Thomas, Redcar Services which provided public transport through Southborough to Tonbridge and Tunbridge Wells, as well as to other towns and villages.

I joined Redcar the year after James set up the business in 1923. He was a local man, educated at Tonbridge School, after which he was, for a short time, with the South-eastern Railway, studying mechanical engineering. When the war broke out he served with the Special Rifle Brigade, and then joined the Flying Corps, taking his pilot's certificate in 1915. He gained the rank of major.

He could be very brusque, presumably a result of his military service. In fact, his brother Yule came to see me after I'd been interviewed for a job as a shorthand typist but

A cartoon from the Courier *from 1924 showing the profitability of Redcar Buses.*

James Bogue Elliott.

before starting to work for them, and asked : 'Did I frighten easily?' I replied: 'Whatever do you mean?' He said that his brother, James, who was the managing director, could be quite frightening but if you stood up to him he was all right! Apart from my holiday each year, I had to work everyday except Christmas Day – I even used to go in on Good Friday and open the post.

In fact, those who worked for Redcar were really happy to do so and James, Yule and Thomas were highly respected. I remember one year, 1926, that the outdoor staff wanted to show their appreciation of their boss and they had got a subscription up and presented James with a silver cigarette case and silver match box. This was presented to

him at the annual outing – in fact, there were two outings each year. Half the staff went one week, the other half the next. Three coaches would take about eighty-five each time up to London for a lunch at the Regent Palace Hotel and then we would go to the Palladium for a show.

There was great rivalry between Redcar and Autocar for passengers. One of our advertising slogans was 'All the way for a jam jar', meaning you could go anywhere on the route for a penny. In 1924 Redcar had a fleet of nineteen buses and carried 1,537,063 passengers and made a profit of £2,625. When the Greenline came on the scene, competition was even fiercer. Redcar was taken over by Maidstone and District in 1935.

We had a Grand Reunion and Smoking Concert for ex-Redcar employees at the Friendly Societies' Hall in Camden Road, Tunbridge Wells in January 1951. Tickets cost 5s 6d. I've still got the souvenir menu and programme. There was a buffet of ham and tongue sandwiches, bridge rolls, salmon pasties, sardine and anchovy and cheese savouries, stuffed celery, sausage rolls, mince pies, trifles, jellies, pastries and tea or coffee. The entertainment consisted of a band, the 'Revd Rustus Peabody' – a recitation, I think – the Black Aces, Larry Seymour, an accordionist, Ernie and Harry. We ended up with community singing and the National Anthem – God Save the King.

On the Council

Charles S. Clements, known as Charlie, worked for the Southborough Urban District Council for many years and he recalls some of the others, mostly clerks and surveyors, who were there in the 1940s and 1950s.

My late father-in-law, Walter Churn, was a councillor for quite a few years. He was also very active in the Men's Club and the British Legion, being a veteran cavalryman from the First World War. His daughter, Dorothy, was a secretary in the office of Mr Wood, the Town Clerk, until I married her in 1950.

I worked with Henry Hayes for nearly fifteen years. He had served in the wartime RAF as a pilot officer in Bomber Command and was awarded the DSO. Henry and his crew had just taken off one night with his flight when his aircraft developed a fault. Henry had to make a forced landing with his crew and a load of bombs. The landing took in two or three fields before they came to a halt. His rear gunner was killed by the impact but the bombs fortunately did not go off.

Then there was Tony Friend, the draughtsman, who had been a 'Desert Rat'. He drove a tank in the Western Desert and, one morning, he and the crew were taken prisoner by the German Afrika Korps. Later in the day they managed to escape and, on foot, made it back to the Allied lines by nightfall. After demob and joining the Council, Tony decided to take driving lessons. He failed his first test miserably, probably because he argued with the examiner. He thought that driving a tank in the desert was sufficient qualification to drive a car in Southborough – how wrong could he be!

Freddy Keel was Assistant Clerk for many years and was later Town Clerk. He won the Military Medal in the Second World War and is remembered in the name of Keel Gardens. Another member of the Clerk's office was Freddy Pierce, a very popular chap and *the* authority on High Brooms, where little happened without his knowledge. Last,

but certainly not least, there was Graham Pentecost, who served the Council for forty-nine years.

The saga of Holden Pond and the arrival of the ducks comes to mind. It was decided in the 1950s to construct a small island with a duck house. Tom Scott, Bob Wheeler and Dick Linnington built a raft of barrels lashed together and Dick sailed off into the pond to find a suitable place for the island. Sadly, the raft was somewhat unstable and the sailor was tipped into the pond at a point where, at the time, there was a deep hole. He surfaced, minus specs, and I suppose they still repose there somewhere in the mud. However the island and house was duly built and two ducks were bought from Tonbridge market. These were introduced to the water and promptly sank to the bottom. The water, was, fortunately not all that deep and they lived to see *terra firma* again. No-one informed us that not all ducks swim, and these had either not preened themselves or had no oil in their feathers anyway!

No account of the Council as it was years ago would be complete without mention of the outdoor staff, headed for many years by Ernie King, the Council foreman, father of Ron King. He deserves credit for his dedication to duty at the time of snow clearing; whatever the time of day or night, he had his merry band out with shovels and snowploughs. Not only roads but also pavements were promptly dealt with, which is certainly not the case now. Furthermore, the foul and storm water sewers and manholes were not too well documented, especially across the Common, and Ernie was a mine of information on these important details. I cannot imagine what happened when he left the scene – by then I had 'deserted' to the Borough Council.

In 1948 or 1949, the Council had, in

'Judder' Heasman with 'Old Tom', with the equipment used for clearing drains and emptying cesspits.

addition to the refuse lorry, a cart, a sort of tumbrel, drawn by an elderly cart horse, Old Tom, and driven by 'Judder' Heasman, but both had reached the end of the road. 'Judder' was pensioned off, but poor Old Tom went to the knacker's yard. That day was a very sad one in the office – even Tom Scott, the surveyor, showed some emotion.

For years we had a road sweep, Charlie Allcorn; quite a character, that one. He was always in a hurry to get the job done and was a pain in the neck to his unfortunate assistants, who had to keep up with him. They were more laid back and saw no reason to hurry, there was always tomorrow. In his spare time, Charlie brewed beer in his little terraced cottage, where Hythe Close now

stands. His brewery was not particularly hygienic but the beer was quite palatable. Another sweeper swept the passage beside the Flying Dutchman or, as he preferred to write on his time sheet, 'sweeping the passed'. The spelling was original but the 'passed' was always clean and tidy.

There were big changes in local government when the Planning and Health Acts of 1947 came into force the following year. These Acts were very complex and quite a challenge for a small Council like ours. Licences for house building had to be dealt with. This was 'fun', as there was a rash of applications for granny-flats, house additions for elderly relatives. In most cases, the grannies failed to materialise and the flats were then sold off at grossly inflated so-called 'market prices'.

Although the Health Act was rather daunting to administer, it did eliminate one of the sights we used to see, a queue outside the Council offices – in full view of passers-by – of people waiting to receive Poor Law Relief. It also meant that the general public could receive hospital treatment without an interrogation from the Almoner, who had to decide whether your financial position justified paying for the treatment.

Our work was extremely varied, anything from queries on the new legislation to complaints, genuine or otherwise, and there lay the seamy side. A certain old lady who lived in Taylor Street was eccentric, to put it mildly, and she had a delusion that she was being watched all the time. She claimed that folk peered through her windows upstairs and downstairs and, on autumn and winter evenings, the searchlights from the Army unit still operating near the Royal Oak Inn on Speldhurst Road were directing beams into her cottage windows – actually an impossibility.

However, her complaints were duly noted by the Council, usually me, but with fast thinking it was decided to call it a 'Defence' matter and she was told to go to the police, then occupying premises at the corner of Meadow Road and London Road. The police response was: 'Oh, no, you must go to the Council offices' and so it went on and on for months. There was one occasion when the poor old lady was seen approaching the surveyor's office, whereupon one of us locked the street door, the surveyor dived into his inner sanctum and the rest of us hid under our desks. After trying the door and peering through the window, she departed and we re-surfaced. To use modern jargon, it was not very 'customer friendly' but it was a wearing time.

Making Cricket Balls

Alec Brown is 'well over eighty' but looks twenty years younger than that; he lives in Holden Corner, overlooking the pond, in the house where he was born. He married his wife Katey in April 1936. They first met when they were both seventeen; Katey was working for the Fleming family who lived in Bentham House (the owner was the brother of Sir Alexander Fleming, the bacteriologist and discoverer of penicillin). Alec is still active and keeps fit by touching his toes seven times everyday after he comes downstairs each morning. For all of his working life Alec was a cricket ball maker, working for Tworts in Park Road and then for Dukes at Chiddingstone Causeway (now British Cricket Balls at Beltring).

Alec Brown with his dog, Nibbs, in 1946.

Alec Brown, cricket ball maker of Holden Corner, in 2000.

Southborough Rifle Club, winners of the Cup and Shield, 1920/21. From left to right, back row: Tom Barden, Baden Hartridge, Alfred Bachelor, Victor Twort, -?-, Vic Tanner, -?-, -?-, Frank Hartridge. Front row: W.F.A. Cox, Charles Tingley, ? Petty, -?-, -?-, Herbert Silver, Edwin Twort (the cricket ball maker).

I was lucky to have been born with long fingers which meant that I could stitch the cricket balls quite well. We used to be paid piece work when I first started but later on we were paid task work.

Bernard Best was the nearest to anybody who I've seen who was automatic. He would just sit there all day working away at stitching; he was the fastest too although his work, I must say, was a bit rough. In eight hours, he could stitch ten balls.

Edwin Twort was the owner of the business and he was well known for being tight. He wouldn't pay us for the two-minute silence on Armistice Day. When I first started, we worked away under oil lamps but then electricity was introduced. Edwin charged his workers threehalfpence a week each to pay for it. Two of us held

out, but eventually we had to pay up. A lady called Edie worked for the Tworts in the house; she got told off by Edwin for peeling the potatoes too thickly!

The best that can be said about Edwin was that he was a modern gentleman trying to run a firm on Victorian lines. One worker, Fred Rosewell, got stood off for a week for smoking when he shouldn't have. In fact, he wasn't smoking; he just had a roll-up ready behind his ear for when the smoke break came.

Henry Oliver was a quilt winder; he would make the middle of the balls by winding worsted around a cork core. He was deaf and you really had to shout in one ear to make him hear what you were saying. Once Edwin came into the workshop and shouted into Henry's good ear: 'You owe me a ha'penny!' Henry said: 'What?' 'You owe me a ha'penny – and it's cost me a penny to come and collect it!'

Edwin's son Thomas took over the business. Thomas was not so mean. He treated me and my wife to a show in London – *The Sound of Music* – after I had worked there for forty years. He also treated the workers, not with wives, to a dinner at the Weavers to celebrate the firm's hundred years in business. I can't remember what we ate, probably leg of liver and buffalo chips!

Sid and Bill Woodhams came to work for Tworts. Bill had no teeth so wore false ones but they gave him so much trouble that one day he took them out and put a chopper through them. His gums were so hard though, he could eat an apple. Bill could sleep anywhere and would often stretch out on the floor during a break.

One day when he was asleep we decided to carry him out and leave him in the road but he woke up as we carried him out the door.

Amos Eade used to say that he lived fifty years to please people and that he would live another fifty years to annoy them. But he was found in Bidborough pond with a bottle of whisky in his pocket – it was the second time, the first time he was pulled out alive but this time he drowned.

I did five and a half years in the RA on searchlights during the war and was on Bath race course waiting to go abroad when the V2 landed in Park Road, causing considerable damage to buildings including the Twort factory at Number 28A. Katey and our son Alan were living in Park Road at the time and after the explosion they both went to my parents' house in Holden Corner, in the middle of

Holden Pond in a watercolour from 1878.

Near Southborough,
Tunbridge Wells, 1878

A V2 rocket exploded in Park Road, Southborough, on Monday 13 November 1944 at 22.47hrs. Fortunately no-one died as a result of this incident, although six people were taken to hospital, including the occupants of the house in the background. The man on the left in the trilby is Henry Farmer, a cricket ball manufacturer and former captain of Southborough Cricket Club. (Photograph from Doodlebugs and Rockets *by Bob Ogley)*

the night, as they were bombed out. When my father opened the door to them, he said: 'Whatever's happened to you? You look like a couple of sweeps.'

When *What's My Line?* was on television with Katie Boyle, Joe Woodrow and I went up to the BBC Lime Grove studios and we beat the panel. They never did guess we were cricket ball makers. Tom Twort said to me before going up to London to film the programme: 'Make sure you've got plenty of money with you as I hear the canteen there is very good.'

John Hudgell, who now lives in Hythe, Kent, was also a cricket ball maker at Tworts and remembers the V2 incident.

The next day we tried to retrieve our tools from the rubble of the building. Roy Cavie, Henry Farmer and Amos Eade were among those looking for their personal tools because without them you could not work. Amos dived into the collapsed building and found his and went off to work for one of the Tonbridge ball makers.

Ernest Batchelor was the foreman of the firm at that time and he used to live on the London Road opposite the top of Pennington Road. When I found that the factory had gone I went to find him and he was sweeping up the broken glass from his windows. We went back to the factory and rescued the contents of the safe as Ernie had a set of keys.

Harry Dent was in the RAF at this time but used to visit the ball firm when on leave. We became firm and lifelong friends. I joined the RAF soon after the rocket episode. After the war Harry and I played badminton and tennis together as a men's pair and represented Southborough in the Tunbridge Wells League. Harry was an extremely fine games player. In later years he became Mayor of Southborough (1983-1984) and took a meeting of the Town Council only days before he died of cancer. Southborough Bowls Club has a Harry Dent cup they play for every year.

Hello Girls

In May 1999 several telephonists from the Southborough Exchange got together at Barbara Boorman's house to reminisce. They included Ivy Ashby, Pat McCombe (née Clifton), Margaret Heath (née Couchman), Maureen Wallis (née Chapman), Wendy Thomson (née Streeton), Joyce Woodruff and Barbara Sellins (née Huggett).

There were six operating positions in the exchange with about 2,000 subscribers, including those families who shared a line. If you wanted to make a call and picked up the phone and somebody was already talking you had to wait until they had finished.

The day operators would work from 8 a.m. to 8 p.m. and Mr and Mrs Coppinger were the caretaker operators overnight. In 1951 pay was £2 4s a week. Barbara Boorman became a telephonist at this time; her first job had been with the baker's Paine, Smith where she was paid £1 2s 6d a week, so her new job was double what she had been earning.

Pat McCombe remembers that she was on duty over the Bank Holiday weekend in 1956 when a severe hailstorm disrupted

Holden Pond in 2000.

Southborough telephone operators in June 1954. From left to right: Margaret Martin, -?-, Margaret Heath, -?-, Daphne Hooker, Di Norman, Jean Rudge, Ethel Cocks.

everything. Everybody wanted to phone to check and see that their friends and family were all right and Pat's supervisor said she could get her fiancée to come in and help her because of the extra work. Peter Dews was a telephone engineer and knew how to operate the phones.

All the telephonists had to sign the Official Secrets Act, as civil servants, and agree to not listen in to, or talk about, any calls or callers. They are still bound to this vow of secrecy which will continue to well into the twenty-first century. Some calls were designated 'PUT' which stood for 'permanently uninterrupted transmission' – those from Eridge Park to the Royal Family were PUT calls as were those from Chartwell, Churchill's home. We had to put 'scramblers' on sensitive calls.

Most of the girls cycled to work and thought nothing of getting on their bikes and cycling to Paddock Wood or any other local exchange if they were short staffed.

There were loads of 'chat ups' because, like nurses, everyone assumed they were young and single. Every month there were dances at West Malling RAF Station and a coach would be sent to take the girls over for the evening. If we were working on a Sunday then the Army camp at the Warren in Crowborough would call an operator and then put the phone next to the wireless so that we could listen to Family Favourites.

The supervisors were very strict; if you were late for work you were fined and money taken out of your wages. Ivy remembers being late for work one day when her train was derailed – she was docked 3s 6d. There was no food or drink while you were working. We did have a rest room for tea and snacks; there was a small cooker in there and one year we managed to cook a turkey in it.

We would often take messages from subscribers like: 'I'm just popping out for ten minutes so please tell anybody who calls to phone again later'. Once an old lady phoned and said that she was going away for two weeks and so it was all right for me to take a holiday. Some subscribers really thought there was one operator for each house!

Working for the Corporation

Mr Kennard of Laundry Cottage, Pell Green, Wadhurst, lived and worked in High Brooms in the 1930s at first as casual labour potato picking and then for the Corporation in the Sewage Works situated just over the boundary in Tunbridge Wells.

The brickyard was the chief source of work for a lot of the High Brooms men and a laundry job was common for the women. I remember going down under the railway bridge. I recall there was a couple of houses, one on the right and a little lock-up shop

The 'hello girls' at Southborough exchange in 1963. From left to right: Mrs Coppinger, Margaret Jordan, Monica Marsh, Joyce Woodruff, Judy Bellingham, Pauline Brown, Wendy Thompson, Sue Whitlock. The exchange closed when Subscriber Trunk Dialling arrived in Tunbridge Wells on 20 February 1965, when the new automatic exchange costing £2½ million opened in St John's Road.

The staff of the Royal Kent Laundry in North Farm Lane, High Brooms, c. 1945.

selling baccy, sweets, etc. An old chap by the name of Churchill and his sister ran it. Very handy for brickyard chaps. Makes the mind boggle when you think of fags – Woodbines, Park Drive etc. at fourpence for ten. Opposite was a double dwelling; old Mr Bridges lived in one half and his son, Bill, in the other. The road that ran up to the Sewage Works on the left and rubbish tip on the right was called Tanks Hill. This road joined Lamberts Road and a little way along that was Armstrong's Orchid Nurseries.

Some of the Corporation workers I remember were Harry Beadle, Bert Parkes (foreman), Bert Jeffery, Jack Carter, Ern Large, Bert Dadson and Bill Bridges. North Farm, Home Farm and Sewage Fields had been part of the Colebrook Park Estate which joined on to Summerhill in Tonbridge. In the 1930s the big house was empty and Frank Woodhams and his wife were gardener-caretakers. Another brother Arthur was the keeper and the shooting was let to a Colonel Grey from Cranbrook. Pheasants were reared in those days in the old way under cluck hens. They were so tame that we had a great difficulty getting them into the air for the guns. I used to help Arthur Woodhams on shoot days. I have known the time when you would practically push them to get 'em to fly.

High Brooms in those days had a few inhabitants who were fond of a bit of roast pheasant. On a few occasions I would hear the crack of a .410, one for the pot so to speak. Once a new copper came to live in Silverdale Road and his beat took in the Home Farm. He heard the crack of a .410 walking around one day and thought he would feel the collar of one of the poachers. They heard him coming and took off over the sewage fields which they knew were crossed with ditches that used to flood with sewage. The copper, of course, did not know the lie of the land and finished up in one of them. Some of the locals grinned. It was said that the air over Silverdale was blue when his missus saw the state of him when he went home.

Bentham Farm

Philip Sale grew up in Southborough and remembers helping on Bentham Farm when the three Penticost brothers ran it as a dairy farm.

There was Percy, Spencer and Frank Penticost. I would help Percy with the hay making and used to catch mice and rats as the grass was cut. As well as cows on the farm, they also had some pigs and I used to pick through the broken biscuits which were fed to the pigs, looking for the chocolate ones which I would eat myself.

Spencer was deaf and used to push the milk trolley to the houses in Southborough and ladle out the milk. Frank was the taciturn one, who always wore a trilby hat; he almost took his thumb off once when a swop hook glanced off a stone. Mr Wood was the cowman and he had a big drooping moustache.

My uncle Will lived in Holden Corner and in the 1920s there were fields at the back – what is now Manor Road was a very steep field and the cows used to slip down the hill when it was wet. My uncle used to kill wasps' nests, if they were a nuisance, with cyanide. The workers who were building the Council houses had a hut and they would throw their empty condensed milk tins away. This attracted the wasps and uncle Will and I located their nest. After we killed it with cyanide we dug it out. It was as big as I was and I remember baking layers of the nest, as big as a long-playing record, in

Bentham Farm, Modest Corner.

Emily Harris (widow of Charlie, who was a gardener at Bentham House) is on the left and her sister, Mary Willard, on the right. The little girl is Pat Sale (now Ballard). The photograph was taken at the back of Wood Cottage; note the fig tree growing against the wall.

Numbers 1 and 2 Wood Cottage.

the oven for half an hour and then using the grubs as bait to fish in Holden Pond. Roast wasp grubs made a very pleasant smell.

Back when Pontius was a Pilot, Mrs Petty ran the shop in Holden Corner and I used to pop in for a penny's worth of sweets. When I went over to Modest Corner to get milk from the Penticost Dairy at Number 10, I would sometimes get sweets in the shop on the corner with Victoria Road run by Mr Skinner. I loved going to the dairy and seeing Edie with her rosy cheeks and great big smile and white bobbly hat working with the big bowls and jugs. The Penticosts used to have a stuffed fox, two little owls and a pheasant in a glass case.

My aunt and uncle, Emily and Charles Harris, used to live in 2 Wood Cottage. He was a gardener to Mr Pott at Bentham House and when he died Emily's sister, Mary Willard, moved in. The water for the house came from a spring-fed well under the oak tree in the garden. There was no concrete path to the house: just cinders from the stove that was in the modern room on the right side of the house. There were vegetables and fruit bushes in the garden, front and back – loganberries, gooseberries and raspberries – and they kept chickens. At the back of the cottage a big fig tree grew up the wall.

I remember watching Mr Reeves the blacksmith at the top of Holden Road doing the horses' feet when they came in to get new shoes. Terrier dogs used to nip in and steal the hoof parings – they especially liked the bits that had been singed by the red hot iron.

Town Clerk

Graham Pentecost worked for forty-nine years for Southborough Urban District Council. For the last twenty-five years, until his retirement in 1997, he was the Town Clerk.

Bentham Hill House.

I was born in Nursery Road, High Brooms and always considered myself a High Broomer, or treacle miner, as others used to call us. My father was a painter and decorator and my grandfather was the road sweeper in High Brooms. I played all my football for High Brooms, first for the Old Boys and then for the Casuals and I didn't even really know where Southborough was until I got a job there.

I went to the Boys' School and remember watching the Battle of Britain fought in the skies above us and the tinkle of the spent bullets as they fell out of the sky. The V1 that came down in the allotment was exciting. We had watched a Spitfire tip it off course with its wing and for a time it wandered all round the sky before landing without exploding. It was lunch time and there were no teachers around and all of us boys made our own way to the air raid shelters when we saw the bomb was coming

our way. I remember the headmaster, Mr Bryson, complimenting the whole school for the orderly way we had taken shelter.

As boys we used to play in Brokes Wood and along the stream there which we always called the Brook. We used to swim in the lily pond and I remember getting a drink of coffee from the Italian prisoners of war who were working in the wood, cutting pit props. The prisoners wore brown uniforms with distinctive patches on their backs. They weren't allowed to use public transport but walked around quite freely.

I went to the Boys' Tech in St John's and left when I was sixteen. A chance meeting in Yew Tree Road with my old headmaster saw me go along to the Southborough offices as he told me there was a job as assistant clerk going. I really wanted to work on a farm but my father told me it 'was regular work with a pension at the end of it'.

When I arrived in Southborough, Ern

King, father of Ron, was the foreman of the outside workers. Bill Kember was the treasurer, Freddy Keel was the clerk and Freddy Pierce his deputy, and Thomas Albert Scott, known as Scottie, was the surveyor and engineer.

The only thing I really regret is not getting Listed Building status for the old showroom of the High Brooms Brickworks and for the foremen's houses on North Farm Road. I thought the showroom would make a fine little brickwork museum. Sir Hugh Casson came into the office one day when he was working on David Salomons to secure Listed Building status for that, and I tried to persuade him that High Brooms also had some worthy buildings.

Graham Pentecost, town clerk for nearly fifty years.

Rejected bricks from the brickworks were used in this wall.

A heron finial on the brickworks' foremen's houses in North Farm Road.

The former training centre of High Brooms Brickworks. It is now the reception centre for P.K. Motors.

Lee of P.K. Motors in their workshop, which used to be the showroom for High Brooms Brickworks.

CHAPTER 5
Wartime

Clappie

Miss E.C. Clapson used to live at 27 Charles Street. Everyone knew her as 'Clappie'. Her corsets creaked like mad. She never had electricity or water in her house but used candles and paraffin lamps and two wells in the back garden. She wrote a poem called Doodlebug Alley.

How we saved the paper and the cardboard
               and the bones
Is another picture of the war for homes;
Bags and tins and bottles, jars and iron too.
Each of these were needed, so we saved
               those too.
Next they took our gates and our iron fences
To make tanks to shell Germany's defences,
Big bombs falling, thudding, whistling on
               their way
How we shook for terror, longing for the day,
Walking in the darkness in the winter
               nights,
Bumping into people, trees and walls (no
               lights).
What with yelling sirens moaning in the
               night

Miss E.C. Clapson ('Clappie') in the garden of 27 Charles Street. She wrote Doodlebug Alley.

Making all our dreams and slumbers take
their flight.
Doodles chasing o'er us with their fiery tails
Shaking doors and windows in their wicked
trails.
Crashing on the peaceful farms and woods
and towns,
Leaving them with sorrow, death and rubble
mounds.
How we dodged the shrapnel falling in the
street,
Broken glass from windows flying round our
feet.
Eighty days and nights of terror, danger, fear,
Never knowing any moment if our end were
near.
Flying bombs by thousands sent us by our
foe,
Moaning doodle-doodle-doodle as they go.
O what clever airmen fighting for our lives,
Thinking nought of danger in their many
dives.
Great guns roaring overhead dare not tarry,
For this was the famous 'Doodle-Bug Alley'.
O what many dangers God has brought us
through,
May we live to praise Him, trust Him always
too.

Wartime Memories

*Edward Thomas Culmer, always known as
Ted, attended St Peter's Boys' School on the
Common in the 1920s. When war came he
enlisted in the Queen's Own Royal West
Kent Regiment and his battalion was part of
the British Expeditionary Force that was sent
to France at the beginning of hostilities; by
then he was a lance corporal. Trevor Culmer,
Ted's son, takes up the story of how his father
was awarded the Military Medal.*

During the retreat to Dunkirk in May
1940 my father and his men were defending
a house that they had occupied in
Oudenarde. There were several air raids that
day and during one of them an incendiary
bomb came through the roof of the house.
Without hesitation, my father sprang
forward and threw the bomb out of the
window, thereby probably saving the lives of
his men. I've still got the medal that he was
awarded for this.

Later in the war the 4th Battalion of the
regiment was in Burma and fought
heroically against the Japanese. Some of the
fiercest fighting was at Kohima, where some
500 men, including my father, defended the
position against an estimated 9,000
Japanese for fifteen days. The battalion lost
61 killed in action, 125 wounded and 13
missing. During the defence of Kohima, the
men of the Royal West Kents repulsed
twenty-five major enemy attacks and
inflicted well over 1,000 casualties on the
Japanese. This staunch defence had also
averted a catastrophe – by preventing the
advance of the 31st Japanese Division for
fifteen days, this had allowed the 2nd British
and 7th Indian Divisions to arrive in the
battle area and prevent the invasion of
India.

The official history of the regiment states:
'much of the praise for the successful
outcome of this siege must, as often in the
story of the British Army, be given to the
private soldiers and the junior leaders. This
was indeed a "soldiers' battle". Hand-to-
hand skirmishes were fought practically
every night, and time after time the brave
and skilful deeds of a section or platoon
commander prevented disaster. Many of the
troops who were not counted as casualties
had in fact been slightly wounded or
concussed by blast, and a number of the less

Ted Culmer in the uniform of the Queen's Own Royal West Kent Regiment, 1940.

Malcolm, the grave digger in Southborough cemetery, standing by the grave of Pilot Officer John Brady, killed in action in 1940.

seriously wounded had returned to their posts because the field hospital was already full. As the days passed the platoons and sections got smaller and smaller. At the end, one platoon consisted of a single private. He asked, with a grin, if he could put a "pip" up.' After the war, Ted came back to live in Southborough and worked in the Kelsey Brewery along St John's Road in Tunbridge Wells.

Jack Avis has a very poignant memory of the Second World War.

My father used to work in the wholesale

grocers that was in Baysinghall Lane in Tunbridge Wells. I'll never forget my tenth birthday – September 13th 1940 – a German bomber, unable to find its target in London flew over Tunbridge Wells and dropped a string of bombs. The place where my father worked received a direct hit and he was killed. At that time we used to live in 10 Prospect Road. So whereas it is true to say that nobody was killed in Southborough during the war, one Southborough resident was definitely killed, albeit just a couple of miles away.

Mrs Jill Wickens (née Grove) lives in Chestnut Avenue now but during the war she lived at the bottom of Edward Street, in a stone cottage that had been built for one of Sir David Salomon's workers.

As a child we used to play outdoors all the time. Sometimes we used to take food to a man living in the old quarry opposite Kibbles Lane. We thought he was a spy, most likely a double agent.

Next door to us at 99 Edward Street lived Bernard and Daisy Brady and their family. Their son Bernard John Richard, who we called John, went to The Skinners' School from 1930 to1936. He was in Knott House. Even at school he was mad keen to join the RAF but, of course, he was too young. Once he borrowed an umbrella from my sister and jumped out of his first floor window using the umbrella as a parachute! He broke his leg. When he was old enough he joined up and became a pilot officer in 615 Squadron which was part of the BEF and took part in defending the retreat of the soldiers as they were evacuated from Dunkirk. The squadron lost twenty-five Hurricanes in France. John was shot down and injured in June 1940 and he died two months later back in England. He's

Bernard · John · Brady

Born   December 21st. 1919.
At School 18·9·30 ~ 1·4·36.
·KNOTT HOUSE·
·R · A · F ·
FLYING OFFICER.
Killed on Active Service.

A memorial to John Brady in the Skinners' School Book of Remembrance.

Edward (left) and Fred Eggleson during the Second World War. Flt-Sgt Fred Eggleson was reported missing in action, 2 January 1944.

buried in Southborough cemetery.

George Funnell used to live in Forge Road but retired to Glenrothes, Fife, where he still lives. He remembers his childhood in the 1920s and 1930s, before his service in the Second World War.

My father purchased 13 and 13A Forge Road from his mother for £200 in 1921. He turned No. 13 into a general shop with the help of his mother who owned a shop in Springfield Road. There was little money or work in those days. Woodbine cigarettes were only twopence for five. Lads were sent to the shop with half a penny, for one Woodbine so that Dad could have a smoke. For a farthing one could buy four toffees, whereas most sweets were a ha'penny.

My father made ice cream to sell at a ha'penny and, for the wealthy, one penny a cone. The paper round on a Sunday started in High Brooms, after meeting the paper train from London at 5.30 a.m. We delivered through Southborough, Bidborough, Penshurst and Speldhurst. The journey was made on an old motorbike with a sidecar. The lamps on the first bikes worked with gas from carbide lamps.

One of my first memories was standing watching Mr Carter the blacksmith shoeing the horses owned by Mr George Paine for pulling the bread carts. The horses were stabled in a building at the rear of our house. When I left school, I worked for Mr Paine. I remember Lady Salomons; I knew her chauffeur, Mr Nunn, when I was a lad.

The Cub meetings under Miss Thorogood used to be the highlight of the week. I was permitted to attend the 1931 camp at Felixstowe because my mother was ill. I went with my brother Frank and cousin Wilfred.

I put my age on a year to join a new TA unit in May 1939. It was the 55th Kent Regiment RA. We met twice a week, training on rather new 3.7-inch anti-aircraft guns. Few thought that, a few months later, we would be in Maidstone and District buses, travelling to our first war station on the Isle of Grain. I left the unit and was posted to Division HQ and from there to an Essex regiment at Dover. We used our 3.7-inch guns from the Normandy beaches in 1944 to Hamburg as both AA and against ground targets.

One of my friends was Fred Eggleson who lived at 16 Forge Road. He was a good swimmer and used to go to the Monson Road Baths. After leaving St Peter's School he went as an assistant to Leslie Moon, the butcher. When he was eighteen, he joined the RAF and rose to become a flight sergeant; his brother Edward served in the Royal Navy and a third brother worked on the land. In December 1943, Fred and I went for a drink at the Beehive in Modest Corner. Two weeks later, on January 2nd, he went missing in action. He was twenty-one when he died.

The Crown Inn

Barbara Boorman (née Tingley) is the daughter of Clarrie (Clarence) Tingley who took over the Crown Inn, London Road in 1935 and was still landlord when he died, of cancer, in August 1963. His wife Leonora carried on until October 1964.

The Crown was one of the busiest pubs during the Second World War as it was used by the soldiers who were based at Great Bounds where Nissen huts had been built to house them. As an infant I remember being carried through the pub to kiss the soldiers goodnight. We did not have a spirit licence in those days and only

The north-west corner of Great Bounds in 1933/34, seen from the Park, with the Bounds Oak to the right in the foreground. Soldiers camped in the grounds during the war.

The landlord of the Crown at Southborough, Clarrie (Clarence) Tingley (centre), c. 1958. On the left is Mr Golding and on the right an unknown newspaper artist.

Demolition of Great Bounds. (Courier photograph)

A Cork Club outing from the Crown, Southborough, in 1939. The landlord, Clarence Tingley, and his daughter Barbara are kneeling at the front. Members had to have a cork on them all the time; if challenged by another member of the club and found not to have one in their pocket, they were fined.

sold beer and sometimes we used to run out of that. During air raids my father would take my sister Margaret and me and bundle us down the cellar amongst the barrels of beer, bottles and coal until the 'all clear' sounded. It was rather frightening but we felt safe down there.

The pub was the black market centre for the people of Southborough because of the good contacts Dad had with the soldiers camped on the Common by St Peter's or from the Bounds. We could always get extra butter and sugar from the soldiers and most Sundays we had a roast, unlike other people. We were never short of petrol, thanks to the soldiers who would bury a can of it just off Victoria Road on the Common and my sister Margaret

would keep watch while Dad used to dig it up. The officers' wives used to be put up in the four bedrooms upstairs when they came to visit their husbands. The soldiers were never any trouble. They were all nationalities – Newfoundlanders, Americans, Canadians. Six New Zealanders came to Ethel White's sister's twenty-first in St Thomas's Hall. They had guitars and played songs like 'Deep in the Heart of Texas'. We really did miss 'em when they went.

Margaret was walking one day in Charles Street with our grandmother when a plane flew over. She waved to the pilot who pulled back the cockpit. It was only then that she saw the swastika and it started firing. You couldn't see Margaret

Pupils at St Peter's Girls' School, June 1949. Barbara Tingley is at the left on the middle row.

for dust. One night in the blackout Margaret bumped into a lamp post and said 'sorry!'

I remember one regular customer, Elijah Denton; he had the strength of a heavyweight boxer and would overpower anyone who crossed his path, even burly policemen. I remember my father proudly showing a large dent in the wall of the games room where Elijah had banged his head in rage ... but I don't think he felt it, due to the amount of beer he'd drunk!

It's true about drinking after hours being a common event. The police knew my father's habits. He'd be counting the days takings about midnight and if PCs Burr and Page were on duty he'd be sure to get a couple of taps at the backdoor and they'd have a chat over a free pint and then off they'd go on their rounds, on

foot, of course.

Dad had a special remedy for colds – he used to dissolve salt in hot water and then sniff the steam under a towel. Dad had a hole in his back caused by a bullet in the First World War – it was big enough to put your fingers in. His brother William Jubilee Tingley survived the sinking of HMS *Hythe* and also later at the Front had his hair parted by a bullet which killed the man behind him. He was transferred to the 10th Field Troop of the Royal Engineers supporting the Imperial Camel Corps. He was killed in the Middle East and is buried in Jerusalem War Cemetery. Another brother Sam came home from the First World War to find his wife in prison for child neglect – one of the children had died. The rest were put into the workhouse at Pembury. Granny

Tingley walked over to Pembury and brought them back to 2 Victoria Road where she raised them.

The local postman Sam Tilley would come in every day on his way home from work and quite often my father would say: 'I saw you go off on your bike this morning and I hadn't been to bed then'. Dad's great love was cards – cribbage and pontoon. He would play all night once or twice a week with his mates, the likes of Sid White, the butcher, and Mr Baker, the chimney sweep.

Another thing I remember my father saying is that he couldn't walk through Southborough without passing someone who owed him money. They all knew he was a soft touch.

Once my sister Margaret was having a piano lesson with our uncle Jack at Langton. Dad came in and said: 'Oh, stop that noise. I can fart better than that!'

Once the doctor came round with a sick chicken and asked my father what was wrong with it. Dad said it had diphtheric throat, told the doctor there was no cure and wrung its neck and put it on the floor where it promptly ran around the room for a while before dropping down dead!

The Cork Club outing usually went to Southend or to see Charlton play football. They always used to play 'penny on the wheel' – making a chalk mark and writing your initials. When the coach came to a stop, the one whose mark was nearest the top would win the money.

Mr Foreman had a yard and stables in Sheffield Road. One day he brought a fox into the pub and let it run around between the glasses and bottles. He also kept a goat and I remember once it ate all around Margaret's skirt!

Jock

Alexander Cameron Ross, who most people know as 'Jock', came to live in the area after he left the Army in 1946. He married his pre-war sweetheart and, in the early 1950s, moved to Weare Road, High Brooms, where he still lives. After he was made redundant when the Brickworks closed, Jock went to work at R.N. Carr Ltd, the ironmongers in London Road in 1965. He still works there part time.

I was born in 1917 at Tain, at the southern shore of Dornoch Firth, Easter Ross, about thirty-five miles north of Inverness. In 1933, aged sixteen, I enlisted as a band boy in the Seaforth Highlanders, my local regiment, and after training served with the 2nd Battalion at Dover. Whilst there, I went several times to play my clarinet with the band in the Calverley Grounds, Tunbridge Wells, where I met my future wife, Olive.

When war came I went with my battalion to France, in the usual bandsman's wartime role of stretcher-bearer. In the retreat to the coast, with the 51st Highland Division, I was wounded in the leg, shot through the ankle. Luckily it was a flesh wound and I could clean it with a piece of string, pulling it from one side to the other through the wound. We could see the ships that were supposed to rescue us and take us back to England, off shore, but they couldn't get in to pick us up. We were ordered to surrender at St Valery in June 1940, and I became a prisoner of war. We had to march from the coast to Rouen – I had one boot on and one boot off because of my wound.

In Rouen, I was taken to a French hospital run by nuns and when I recovered, I stayed on as an orderly as I could speak French. I was treated fairly well along with

Prisoners at Colditz. 'Jock' Ross is in the middle of the front row with the glasses; Douglas Bader is behind him with the pipe.

the others – we were given passes so that we could go out, on parole, into the town of Rouen. It would have been easy to cross the border into Vichy France and escape home, but if medical orderlies who were prisoners of war escaped we would have been court-martialled when we got back to England. If we had no patients to look after, then we could try to escape, but our duty was to look after the wounded and sick prisoners.

I used to go into a café in Rouen and play my banjo in return for drinks. I remember once helping the patron change the labels on the champagne bottles in his cellar. The Germans would come in and demand the best champagne, so we took the labels off the most expensive bottles and put them on the cheapest, and vice versa!

In late 1941, I was in Stalag 8 in Silesia and was introduced to Wing Commander Douglas Bader, the legless RAF pilot. When

I first met him he was lying in bed and using an elastic band to flick pellets at flies on the window pane. I wish I'd never volunteered to be his orderly, although it did mean that I didn't have to do other prisoner work. Anyway, when he was sent to the 'bad boys' camp at Colditz, for making himself a nuisance to the Germans, I went with him. We arrived on August 16th 1942. My duties included getting Bader's breakfast for him from the kitchen – we had bread and butter and mint tea. Most of us used the mint tea to shave with, as we could make our own tea from the Red Cross packages that we were sent. These included dried milk, sugar, dried egg, a tin of margarine, Spam and corn beef and we had fifty cigarettes a week. Because of Bader's disability, the Germans allowed him to soak his sore stump legs every day in a hot bath. I had to carry him down two flights of stairs for the bath, then two flights back up again – he would dig his stumps into my sides as I gave him a piggy back and it almost took my breath away. I would sit outside the bathroom for half an hour waiting for him to finish.

After about six months in Colditz, I had the opportunity to be repatriated as a non-combatant. But Bader refused to let me go: 'You came here with me as my lackey and with me you must stay,' he said. All the time I was with him he never once said 'please' or 'thank you'. He always referred to me as 'Ross'. He had no respect for anyone; he was the big 'I am'. It was a good job he wasn't Commanding Officer of the camp as half the prisoners would have been shot.

Life wasn't too bad in Colditz. We knew how the war was progressing because of the clandestine radio which the Germans never discovered – in fact it was only found five years ago when the castle was being renovated. I played in the band, either the saxophone or clarinet, and we would often have concerts. We used to play cards. Once I won 280 German marks, a French wristwatch and a Rolex Oyster watch on a hand of poker. I had a full house – three aces and two kings. The Rolex was the genuine article and would be worth a lot of money today, but I lost it somewhere over Tunbridge Wells Common after the war.

When the war ended in May 1945 all prisoners returned home but, as space was limited on the American aircraft which carried them, all ranks were allowed only small hand luggage. Bader's large wooden

A close-up of 'Jock' Ross and Douglas Bader at Colditz in 1944.

Alexander 'Jock' Ross is at the front, second from the right, at this Colditz prisoner of war concert.

box containing his spare false legs had to be left behind with me. On returning to England, I reported by telephone to Bader, whose first question was: 'Have you got the legs?'. When I replied 'No' and tried to explain, Bader said 'You ——! (expletive deleted)' and slammed down the receiver. I can't tell you what word he used, but it was most crude.

None of the personal luggage left behind, although, carefully labelled, ever made it back to England. In the confusion and chaos at the end of the war it all went missing. Perhaps Bader's spare pair of false legs will one day turn up in a French car boot sale.

Those who knew Bader either loved or loathed him. He could be extremely rude and insensitive, but he was extraordinarily brave. He was emotionally insecure and had a very severe inferiority complex which he countered with being aggressive and over-confident. Apparently it was a result of his

childhood when he was rejected by his mother. Even his second wife said, had she met him much earlier, she would not have liked him. When he said he had mellowed with the years, she wondered what on earth he had been like when younger! In the programme that was made for Channel 4 about Bader in the Secret Lives series, his close friends said that he could be a super guy or an absolute bastard. I know which one of those I would use to describe him!

CHAPTER 6

Recreation

The Brightridge Infants' School in Charles Street, Southborough. It is now a special needs school.

Childhood Games

Mrs Barbara Dickinson now lives in Playden, near Rye but grew up in Southborough and lived here until she married at the age of thirty-two in 1955.

My paternal grandfather was William Draper, who was landlord of the Crown Inn from 1892 to 1915 and then was at the Hare and Hounds, Bidborough, where he died. He was a very good cricketer, I gather, and is featured in the Southborough Cricket Club's Bi-Centenary Book.

My maternal grandfather, Thomas Martin, was a cricket ball maker with Tworts of Park Road. My grandma, Lucy Martin, was a very good cook and worked for the Salomons family, both at Broomhill and at Huntleys, where the daughter, Lady Blunt, and Sir John lived. She was also a voluntary cook during the Great War, when a military hospital was at Park House.

I lived, as a child, on the corner of Edward

The motto above the door of Brightridge Infants' School reads: 'Take fast hold of instruction. Let her not go: keep her, for she is thy life.'

Street and Meadow Road, opposite a little general shop kept by Mr and Mrs Wiles. I walked with my little friends to the Brightridge Infants' School in Charles Street, where Miss Lettie Wells was Headmistress and Miss Julian her assistant. We walked through an alley from Forge Road to Holden Park Road, where the lovely smell of bread came from the bakery, Paine's, as the shop was called then, in 1929. When I left that school, I walked twice a day up to St Peter's Girls' School – down the Tanyard and up a long path over the Common. The Head was Polly Chambers, but my favourite teacher was Jessie Webb. We often used to come home in the afternoon via the gravel pit, where we enjoyed sliding down to the bottom. We also used to climb a tree at the top of the steps from the Tanyard which was known as the 'haygarzle'; others called it the 'Granny Tree'.

In those days we enjoyed playing with our hoops and tops in the road near home. The girls had wooden hoops and sticks and the boys had iron hoops and iron hooks, which made quite a clatter. Sometimes the Walls Ice Cream man came round on his tricycle, ringing his bell, and we perhaps had a penny snow-fruit or snow-cream. It was lovely! The rag-and-bone man came at times, calling out 'Rags, Bottle'r Bones!' There was a street singer who always came before Christmas and sang 'O, where is my boy tonight?' The milk was brought from Penticost's farm at Modest Corner in a pony and cart and was ladled out of a churn into your jug.

Holden pond was another favourite place and, when it was frozen over, the boys and girls used to make slides, which were a bit dangerous, and my little friend Evelyn fell and broke her arm one day and went home whimpering pitifully, accompanied by a very concerned me.

When a bit older, I used to love watching the cricket and other sports which took place up there on the Common. The most exciting were cycle races. The racing bikes went round and round and quite often someone would fall off and once or twice, I remember, the whole lot ended up in a heap! I also remember when the Dagenham Girl Pipers played on the pitch.

Another excitement was Hospital Sunday, when floats paraded through the town to the Common. We liked to see the 'patients' on the floats with bloody bandages around their heads and other ghastly wounds. Different organizations would parade with banners, the Town Band would play and people with buckets would collect from the crowd for the local hospital. People watching from upstairs were accosted with long hollow poles into which they dropped coins, to listen for the clang as the money landed in the bucket below.

The south front of Great Bounds, 1933/34. The grounds were used for stationing soldiers during the Second World War.

When we were children, on Christmas Day, both grandmothers and two aunts would come to tea and, after tea, my father would play the mandolin while my mother played the piano, and an aunt would sing and play 'Roses of Picardy'. I would display my little presents, coconut ice (home-made) would be handed round and, subsequently, the grown-ups had a glass of port. That was the one time in the year when the two sides of the family got together, although we all lived quite close.

My father, Henry Draper, was a cricket ball maker in the winter, working with Stan Burchett and a Mr Farmer in a workshop on London Road, where the Hythe Close flats now are, and in the summer he was an umpire – for some years on the County circuit. He was umpire at the famous match between Kent and Somerset at Taunton, when Jack Hobbs made his 126th and 127th centuries. I have a framed silk score sheet to prove it, and have twice seen him on television when rain has stopped play and they have shown old film of that match.

Soon after my father died, my mother and I moved to Pinewood Gardens. Having learned the piano (at Tunbridge Wells High School, to which I had won a scholarship), I took organ lessons at St Thomas's church with Percy Gibbons, the then (1941) organist and sang in the choir. I was assistant organist from 1941 to when I left Southborough in the middle 1950s.

I belonged to the Southborough Tennis Club during that time. At first we played on a grass court at the southern end of Prospect Road. Charlie Thorpe, the builder, and his family were leading lights, together with Harry and Winnie Dent. In fact, I met my husband at this club, which moved later to a court set back from the London Road, between the Hand and Sceptre and Vauxhall Lane, which may have been privately owned. I also helped run the St Thomas's badminton club, which the Dents again were involved with.

During the Second World War, we gave up one night a week to running a canteen at St Thomas's Hall for the soldiers stationed up at Great Bounds. I can recall the powdered egg which often ended up like leather!

Aston Martin

Mr P.A. Godfrey Phillips, always known as Phil, owned Holden House from 1948 to his death in 1984. I got to know him well when I was a Scout and he was the District Commissioner. It was a great thrill for us boys to be given a lift in his Aston Martin. I remember on one occasion coming back from a Scout camp in Sussex, he pulled out to overtake a lorry and we both noticed that another vehicle was coming in the opposite direction. To my amazement, and horror, he put his foot down! The acceleration was so good that I was pushed back in my seat and we got passed with room to spare. He commented: 'No point in having it, if you don't use it.' Another time, he went straight over a new roundabout; in other words, he didn't go round it. His only comment: 'That wasn't there in my day.' Before moving to Southborough, Phil lived in Tunbridge Wells and was President of Tunbridge Wells Rangers football team. Frank Chapman, who writes the Warwick column for the Kent & Sussex Courier *records another of Phil's driving exploits.*

Tunbridge Wells Rangers beat Gillingham 4-0 in 1939. (Courier photograph)

If superstition has any part in influencing the outcome of a football cup tie, Tunbridge Wells Rangers former president P.A. Godfrey Phillips had every reason to be confident when he drove to Maidstone in 1939 to watch his team play Gillingham in the final of the Kent Senior Cup. He saw all the Rangers' games and often drove some of the players to away matches in his luxurious car.

The Gills, a powerful side who had applied for re-admission to the Third Division, were expected to slaughter the Rangers. So Godfrey Phillips followed the example of Jack Tinn, manager of Portsmouth, who was reputed to guarantee a win if he put on his spats before a match. Godfrey Phillips consulted his personal omen – that if all the traffic lights were in his favour on the way to a game, Rangers would win.

Towns had few traffic lights back then, and Tonbridge had only one set, at the St Stephen's Church junction. There were anxious seconds as the car descended Quarry Hill, but Godfrey Phillips put his foot down and got through just as the lights were about to change to red. He stayed 'on the green' all the way to the Maidstone Athletic Ground, where the final was played, and told anyone who would listen: 'We are going to win.'

In the event it was not even a close-run thing in the Easter Saturday sunshine. The Tunbridge Wells fans went wild with joy to see their heroes in blue and gold hammer the much fancied Gills 4-0.

The 1st Southborough Company Boys' Brigade, 1942. From left to right, back row: Dick Barnaby, -?-, Ted Ellis, Fred Land, Alfred Nickells, Leslie Skinner, Douglas Funnell, Jack Baker. Middle row: George Skinner, Stanley Wood, Dennis Dann, ? Taylor, Donald Young, Hugh Aviss, -?-, Dennis Acott. Front row: Noel Thorpe, Stanley Hodd, Sam Friend, Jack Faircloth (captain), Revd J. Wesley Kirkham, Sidney Acott, Michael Orford, Leslie Friend.

Wartime Childhood

Hugh Aviss, Wally Usherwood and Stan Hodd were in their early teens during the Second World War. They are still friends and get together from time to time. Stan is the only one who still lives in Southborough, now in Forge Road; during the war, he lived in Meadow Road, a few doors away from pop star David Bowie's grandmother, Mrs Burns. Hugh and Wally were at St Peter's School together and went on to the Judd School. Stan and Hugh were both in the 1st Company of the Boys' Brigade attached to the St John's Methodist church in London Road, where the minister was the Revd John Wesley Kirkham.

The war was fun for us kids. For a start in September 1939 they extended the summer holidays as there were a lot of evacuees arriving. Coaches used to bring them to the Victoria Hall and from there they were billeted on families in Southborough. Some would run away and try and walk back to London. At Judd, we had to double up with a whole school from London, Westminster City School.

We would come home for dinner at midday in those days by bicycle. The trick was to pedal like fury and catch a slow lorry at the bottom of Quarry Hill and then let go when it got to Mabledon.

Everyone had bikes and we would for ever be going off to see a crashed plane.

We'd take a packet of sandwiches and a lemonade and go for miles. One plane came down in Fordcombe and a Spitfire crash-landed near the Viaduct. We used to swap live ammunition at school. Most of us collected fag cards and stamps and we would often go to Bidborough, where the Newfoundland troops were stationed, to cadge Canadian stamps.

The Common was great for climbing trees and much less overgrown with holly back then. The Pineys was a favourite place, 'almost British Columbia', remembers Hugh who was born in Canada. We had favourite trees. The 'A Castle' was a hawthorn tree near the steps opposite the Tanyard. The first footholds on that tree were so well used that they used to shine like glass. Mr Chapman was the ranger then and he lived near the forge at the top of Holden Road. You made sure that he didn't catch you with any holly or heather that you'd taken from the Common. To look down from a tree and see Mr Chapman's face looking up was absolutely terrifying!

There were some very rough parts of Southborough in those days. But the kids soon worked out a pecking order – they'd call it bullying today. Hugh was good at athletics – he learned how to run by escaping from kids who were trying to catch him and throw him into a gorse bush. The Tucks were a very rough family who used to live in the cottages opposite the Cross Keys – we were not all Samaritans then and would cross over to the other side to avoid them.

There were seven police, including a sergeant, in Southborough at that time. The police station was at the junction of Meadow Road and London Road. First we had Sergeant Young and then it was Sergeant Flitter. The most feared PC was Bill Burr, and he knew us all. Stan said: 'When I used to walk with my girlfriend to go courting over the Common, PC Burr would always say: "I bet you wish you could eat her and after you get married you will wish you had".' When the soldiers were camped over there it was rather restricting so when they all moved out after D-Day we got the Common back again. One of the sergeants did my father for failing to take the rotor arm from the family car one night. Parachutists could have used it, if there had been an invasion. The thing I remember most about the end of the war is the lights coming back on again. The blackout had been so good for courting!

The games we played all had a season, whether it was fag cards, marbles, iron hoops, roller skating, conkers, whips and tops or fishing at Great Bounds lake or Holden Pond. One brief craze was to ride our bikes backwards, sitting on the handlebars, on the cricket pitch by St Peter's. Once Stan sent his top through a lady's window and she came round when his Dad came home and demanded he pay for the damage. Stan was asked by his Dad if he had put a top through the lady's window and Stan said 'No'. He asked him a second time and Stan said 'No' so Stan's Dad refused to pay for the damage. Later his Dad said: 'Are you sure you didn't put a top through her window?' and Stan again said 'No, not a top – but I put a whip through it!'

At school we used to have to file out of class into the air raid shelters when the siren went. Later when the guns on Quarry Hill were shooting at planes or the V1s, we didn't bother to go to shelters but we used to go under the desk. Once we

The gravel pit on Southborough Common, 1868.

were having a French dictation exam given by Jimmy Procter, the French teacher. The guns going off so many times meant we had plenty of opportunity to correct and change the dictation while under the desks and out of sight.

Everyone had an allotment and grew vegetables. My dad had one at Bidborough Corner. The thing I remember about shopping was queuing up. Once I was given half a crown by my Mum to go and buy something and I remember flipping it the air as I walked along the street. I missed it and the coin went down a drain. We used to call drains 'busters' for some reason. I went back home and told my

Mum and when Dad came home we went back and took the grid off the buster and fished it out.

Few people owned a car in those days; it was something to go home and tell your parents that so-and-so's dad had bought a car. Double-decker buses were often full top and bottom, with people standing downstairs, and would drive by the bus stop without stopping. We often had to let two or three go by without stopping, and sometimes we were late to school as a result. Getting home from Tunbridge Wells after Saturday night cinema could result in not getting on the last bus and having to walk to Southborough.

Joiner's Gang

John Joiner who lived in Springfield Road with his wife Rosemary was well known for his charity work and support of Bonfire Societies. He was born in Lingfield in 1932 and by his early teens he was taking part in Bonfire Society activities in his home village, then East Grinstead and Rye. In around 1972 the Joiner Gang was formed. This consisted of John and Rosemary and their daughter, Susan, and Rosemary's brother, Alan Jupp, who sadly died of cancer in 1988. In 1976 Susan's boyfriend, now husband, Richard Knight, joined the Gang. The most recent addition was John's grandson, Steven, born in 1989, who took part in his first bonfire parade at Rotherfield in 1990, and Samantha, a granddaughter, born in 1994. John died in August 1998. Rosemary tells their story.

When our daughter Susan was three she was very ill in hospital and stayed there some time. John asked the sister how we could repay the hospital and she said the best thing would be to support any of the hospital's charities.

So I made some costumes and we dressed up as clowns and put on make-up to attend carnivals and bonfires carrying upturned umbrellas, buckets and a dust sheet to collect money. Over the years we must have raised over £100,000 with all the money going to charities. We didn't take expenses but did it just for the enjoyment and the help it brings others.

Highlights include opening the fête at Fordcombe with Leslie Crowther in 1974, taking part in the Queen's Jubilee Bonfire in Windsor Great Park in 1977 and singing carols for the Queen in front of Buckingham Palace in 1979. In 1986 we took part in the procession for the opening of the Special Olympic Games in Brighton – it was the first time the Gang collected over £500 in one evening.

For fourteen years, up to 1990, John was chairman of the Tunbridge Wells Carnival. He introduced many fund-raising events during his time as chairman such as Old Time Music Halls, pram races, It's a Knockout, fun runs and a band tattoo to round off the carnival. The bands and majorettes from near and far made the carnival procession one of the biggest in this area. Businesses took part as well as the 1st Queen's Army Cadet Force and several bonfire societies.

When he retired after the 1990 Carnival there was a letter in the *Courier* thanking him for all of his hard work. Its title was: 'Hats off to John'.

John, in lots of ways, was basically a shy man. He was so sensitive to other people's misfortune that he would cry at things that he saw on TV. He had a good sense of humour – if Susan was going to drive into town he would say 'put the rubber lamp posts out!'

The Gang are still working for charity. We start at Rotherfield on August Bank Holiday and continue through to November. The most famous bonfire is the Lewes one on November 5th – we are all members of the Cliffe Society. Fittingly the Sussex Bonfire and Carnival Societies and friends have donated over £4,000 which is to be given to the A&E Ward at the Kent and Sussex Hospital in John's memory.

The Joiner Gang in Pinewood Gardens, Southborough. From left to right: Richard Knight, Rosemary Joiner, Susan Knight, John Joiner.

An Age Concern bus outside the Day Care Centre, Broomhill Park Road.

Day Care Centres

Southborough and High Brooms Day Care Centres – as remembered by Reverend Alan Wagstaff, vicar of St Peter's with Christ Church from 1976 to 1986.

How did it all begin? Like many situations in life it started in the doctor's surgery. I asked Dr Cameron what he considered the greatest need in Southborough. He had been here many years as a GP and had his finger on the pulse of the parish. I was a newly inducted vicar trying to carry out the advice of older and wiser men, not to start changing everything, but to spend the first year listening.

Dr Cameron said Southborough needed a Day Care Centre for the elderly folk in the parish, but there was never money available to fund such a project. The district had three churches, all in good condition and used mostly once a week; somehow this seemed a waste of facilities.

One morning, armed with a layout pad and pencil, I locked myself in Christ Church, took a chair into the pulpit and sat down to survey the situation.

The result of that morning's work I took to Dr Cameron who was very enthusiastic and suggested that Ron King, who was chairman of Age Concern, would be interested. I took the drawing around to Ron. We sat down at a table with a waste paper basket. I prefaced our discussion with the suggestion that, if the idea was unacceptable, the waste paper basket was a suitable receptacle.

The plan that I had sketched showed the church building divided in half by folding doors: a kitchen and office was planned to be built on the side. The font, which had been at the back of the church was to be moved to the entrance to the church at the front. The pews in the back half were to be removed and chairs provided which would be usable in the Day Care Centre. The concept was acceptable and Ron thought it was just what was needed.

The next step was a feasibility study which would be considered by the Diocese. I wrote to the bishop, the Right Reverend R.D. Say, who enthusiastically wrote back with his approval and enclosing a cheque for £5,000 towards architects' fees.

Our own Parochial Church Council was careful in their acceptance. The church treasurer, Major Alan Charlton, was quite anxious. His ruling was: 'you don't lay a single brick until all the money is in.'

Next the Diocesan secretary, Mr Peter Law, advised on the various steps that would be required for the changing of the use of the building. The archdeacon of Tonbridge, the Venerable Richard Mason, was a tower of strength helping with practical advice and suggestions for the alterations.

Raising finance was the next major project. Southborough Rotary Club adopted the project for the following year with a target of £5,000 and other organizations such as Tunbridge Wells Round Table also said they would help. Schools had their own projects, and even old age pensioners gave a week's pension to help oil the wheels.

Money came in from the most unlikely sources. Two parishioners called at the vicarage with a cheque for £10,000 which they said was to be a loan which, after being used to help fund the project, was to be returned to the Parochial Church Council for the use of the parish. The treasurer for the project was the local bank manager Keith Hutton and, supported by a keen committee, things were beginning to move.

One amusing incident was when we were within £10,000 of our target. Godfrey Phillips, a wealthy retired businessman, lived in Holden House and was well known to me so I visited him and made the audacious suggestion that he should lend me £10,000 interest free to be paid back, hopefully, in two years. He said he'd been caught on that one before, adding: 'Why did I come to him?' since he was a Jew and I was a Christian. We parted the best of friends, and me with the cheque for £10,000. Incidentally when I eventually, within two years, paid him back he said he had written the money off and didn't expect to see it again! But he generously added that I could go to him again if in need.

The architect Peter Lloyd was most generous in greatly reducing his fees. So with the money to hand we were able to start work. Management of the Day Care Centre was then handed over to Age Concern and Jo Wheeler was appointed to oversee the internal progress.

It was about this time that a gentleman turned up on my doorstep. His name was Reg Hobbins and he was a retired brass hat from the Civil Service who had been instrumental in setting up the Tunbridge Wells Day Care Centre. He was skilled in company and ecclesiastical law and helped frame the constitution. This was complicated because church law requires that the incumbent must at all times have complete control of the premises and, if any of the orders were contravened, he had the right in law to close the whole thing down.

A consistory court was set up in the vicarage lounge, and attended by the diocesan lawyer, the chancellor of the Diocese, Christ Church wardens and a few other interested parties. The purpose was to clarify certain aspects of the constitution

The Day Care Centre for Age Concern is located inside St Matthew's church, High Brooms.

to make sure that the rights of future incumbents could not be infringed.

From the time the work was commenced to its eventual completion was exactly two years. Aesthetically, it was decided that the Centre was to be made homely and certainly not institutional. The floor was to be carpeted, the ceiling lowered, and a new central heating system installed. The latter was to benefit the church as well – Christ Church had always been a cold building.

The congregation was most patient, and we were still able to worship while the building work went on. Eventually all was completed despite problems with fitting out the kitchen. The opening ceremony, conducted by the Bishop of Rochester, took place on 11 February 1979.

The church was separated from the Centre by plastic folding doors which while functional were not very beautiful. Mrs Renee Lovegrove, who had recently lost her husband, commented that red velvet curtains would look much better. The quotation was £2,000 and to our surprise and delight Renee said 'get on with it', and then footed the bill.

Then I had a call from an elderly gentleman, Mr Kenneth Howell. He had heard what we were doing and asked if he could be involved in the project. Our youth fellowship had decided to fund a minibus to bring the old folks to the Centre and had saved up £2,500 to buy a second-hand vehicle. Ken Howell said we should have a new vehicle and provided £16,500 for this purpose. Stormonts fitted a lift for the disabled free of charge. Now we needed a garage for the minibus. Under the foremanship of Derek Bing, an excellent garage was built beside the church, with labour supplied by male members of the congregation.

The running of the Centre under Jo's leadership flourished and membership was soon over-subscribed. Just about that time

Elsie Davis, who had been a professional cook working at Mabledon – the Church Pastoral Aid Society Conference Centre at the top of Quarry Hill – was due to retire. Elsie came to the centre and set a very high standard of cuisine and at the amazing price of 40p for a truly lavish lunch. The old folk of Southborough were very happy.

But what about High Brooms? St Matthew's church was large enough to accommodate a Day Care Centre but with the division being lengthways. Age Concern said funds would not be available for two centres in Southborough. We explained that a centre in High Brooms would be an extension of the Southborough centre and this was acceptable.

Plans were drawn up and the money came in, and we were ready to go with the blessing of the Diocese and Age Concern and the members of St Matthew's church. About this time the Revd Walter Robbins was appointed as curate to our parish. He was to be based in High Brooms and was made Priest in Charge of St Matthew's. Walter had been an archdeacon in Argentina but also in his previous working life had been a builder. It was therefore quite natural for him to take over and supervise the building programme and he did a good job.

When we needed just £2,000 to complete the work, the widow of Ken Howell readily subscribed what was needed and the project was completed. The old folk at High Brooms were happy too. 'All things had worked together for good.'

St Peter's School won the local schools' athletics competition in 1933. From left to right, standing: Keen, Culmer, Botting, Stone. Sitting: Williams, Bert Smith (captain), Funnell.